## TESTIMONIALS

"This book will be a treasure for all who read it and take its words to heart." —*Elizabeth McAnally,* Newsletter Editor, Forum on Religion and Ecology at Yale

"Cornell invites us, through AUM, into the very source of nature, the fount of universal religious experience, and the essential experience of self. This intriguing book could very well change the way you see everything." —*Garth Gilchrist,* nature writer, storyteller, portrayer of John Muir

"*AUM: The Melody of Love* is a wonderful gift for those seeking an ecological spirituality. In simple and clear language, Joseph Bharat Cornell tells how to listen to the Song of the Universe and, through meditation, how to merge with the Divine Sound. . . . A spiritual gold mine." —*Rev. Karen MacQueen,* Episcopal priest, Founder of Hindu-Episcopal Dialogue, Episcopal Diocese of Los Angeles

"This book will be an inspiration to anyone seeking direct contact with divine love and bliss. Cornell's *AUM: The Melody of Love* will join the select list of simple, practical spiritual guides that anyone, anywhere, regardless of faith or persuasion, will find accessible and life-changing." —*Joseph Selbie,* co-author The Yugas

"Every sentence is so deep and meaningful that I paused many times while reading—not just to assimilate what was written—but because, in that moment, I actually could go within and feel a touch of the divine. *AUM: The Melody of Love* is a precious gift." —*Vidya Dhote,* PhD, microbiologist

"*AUM: The Melody of Love* offers the sincere reader a sacred pathway to an ever-deepening experience of the divine. What one especially feels, reading these pages, is God's love for all of us, His human children, and how much He yearns for us to reunite with Him through the liberating power of AUM." —*Naidhruva Rush, Editor,* Clarity Magazine

"This wonderful book . . . illustrates that people who spend time in wilderness and those who meditate have at least one important thing in common: they know the sound of silence. . . . The Bushmen call it 'the hiss of the stars.' . . . It is also called AUM." —*Vance G. Martin, President, The WILD Foundation*

"*AUM: The Melody of Love* is an extraordinary guide for those who want to live their lives in a world filled with love, wisdom, and benevolent power. The resonating and elucidating words of this book envelop the reader with a powerful sense of clarity and hope." —*Kate Akers, Director, Sharing Nature New Zealand*

"Cornell has written a virtual guidebook, groundbreaking in its exploration of what is typically a mystical subject. He has made AUM comprehensible and accessible. This is a wonderfully insightful and delightful resource that cannot fail to inspire and enlighten its readers."
—*Nayaswami Nefretete Rasheed, PhD*

"Perfect: beautifully written; clearly inspired. It is easy to read, yet so profound. It is uplifting 'beyond imagination of expectancy', and it carried me right into the center of the experiences the author was describing."
—*Shanti Rubenstone, MD*

"*AUM: Melody of Love* was thrilling to read; and one could feel it was written from a level of clear insight, inspiration, and deep devotion. It gave me a deeper understanding of what AUM is and intensified my longing to commune with it." —*Krishnadas LoCicero, teacher and meditation instructor*

"This revolutionary book will become an enduring favorite of many devotees and will take its place on the reference shelf of many spiritual teachers." —*Dana Lynne Andersen, Founder, Academy of Art, Creativity & Consciousness*

"This book is wonderfully uplifting. It speaks to me of an ecstatic union with God." —*Jon Parsons, attorney-at-law, author of* A Fight for Religious Freedom

ABOUT JOSEPH CORNELL'S
NATURE AWARENESS BOOKS

"This man is connected to the heart of our planet, and the Earth's wisdom shines through him." —**New Texas Magazine**

"Reverence and respect for the nature life forces permeates Joseph Cornell's writings. He shares…ways to experience the joy and expansion of being one and at home with our Earth." —**One Earth**, *Findhorn Foundation Magazine*

"Joseph Cornell has a gift for sensitizing others to their natural world—and to their inner world." —*Douglas Wood, author of* Grandad's Prayers of the Earth

"This is absolutely the best awareness of nature book I've ever seen."
—**Whole Earth Review**

"Joseph Cornell is one of the most highly regarded nature educators in the world today." —**Backpacker Magazine**

"*Listening to Nature* offers a doorway to silent contemplation and relaxation. It deserves a space on the shelf next to the writings of John Muir, Aldo Leopold, and other great naturalists." —**Alberta Naturalist**

"*Listening to Nature* is a splendid masterpiece that captures the "Oneness" we are all seeking to achieve with Nature."

—*Tom Brown, Jr., author of* The Tracker

"*Listening to Nature* gives people a dynamic experience of their unity with the natural world. I heartily recommend it to anyone who desires a deeper relationship with the Earth." —*Alaska Natural History Association*

"*Sharing Nature with Children* sparked a worldwide revolution in nature education and became a classic." —*National Association for Interpretation*

"By using the activities . . . the child actually experiences what it is like to be a part of the natural world. I see this little book as a powerful tool in educating children." —*National Audubon Society*

"*Sharing Nature with Children* is the book that many of us have been hoping someone would write. Now, Joseph Cornell, has written it for us, and what a fine job he has done. Here is a real tool to help children experience the oneness, the beauty and wonder of being in touch with God through His earth." —*Edgar Cayce's* **A. R. E. Journal**

"I found *Sharing Nature with Children* a most original and imaginative concept in a field which is vital for the welfare of the planet." —*Sir Peter Scott*

"Joseph Cornell brings John Muir's voice to children with purity and grace, in words that carry the spirit, enthusiasm and wonder that Muir felt and shared with all. Muir and Cornell are great natural collaborators across the centuries." —*Cheryl Charles, President and Co-Founder, Children & Nature Network*

"*John Muir: My Life with Nature* will convince parents and teachers that contact with Nature is essential to mold children's souls.."

—*ECO Association for Environmental Studies, Brazil*

# AUM

*The Melody of Love*

# AUM

## *The Melody of Love*

### THE SPIRIT BEHIND ALL CREATION

Joseph Bharat Cornell

**Crystal Clarity Publishers**
Nevada City, CA 95959-8599

Copyright © 2013 by
Joseph Bharat Cornell
All Rights Reserved.

Printed in China

ISBN: 978-1-56589-254-5
ePub ISBN: 978-1-56589-517-1

1 3 5 7 9 10 8 6 4 2

*Cover and interior designed by*
Tejindra Scott Tully

Library of Congress
Cataloging-in-Publication
Data *forthcoming*

---

**Also by Joseph Bharat Cornell**

Listening to Nature
John Muir: My Life with Nature
Sharing Nature with Children

---

www.crystalclarity.com
clarity@crystalclarity.com
800-424-1055

DEDICATED TO HOLY AUM
*who animates all creation and speaks to us
through the great saints of all religions.*

*I would like especially to honor the crystal clear
teachings of my Guru, **Paramhansa Yogananda**,
and my teacher, **Swami Kriyananda**.*

# TABLE OF CONTENTS

# FOREWORD

I have known Nayaswami Bharat for nearly forty years, our main association being fellow spiritual seekers and friends. During nearly all of that time he has been a teacher, author, and deep practitioner of the art of meditation. We have both lived most of our adult lives in Ananda Village, one of the foremost spiritual communities in the world. Ananda, now in its forty-fourth year, is a living laboratory for meditation and other spiritual practices. Here we have been able to observe several hundred residents and thousand of visitors, and seen for ourselves the immense benefits gained through daily deep meditation.

Bharat has a genius for finding the essence of a subject, explaining it in clear and compelling ways, and then giving the reader creative exercises to gain an actual experience for himself. This ability is what has given him an international reputation as one of the foremost nature educators in the world, with a well-known society honoring him as one of the "hundred guardian angels of the planet."

In this book he writes about the vibratory essence of creation, known to all religions, and called variously the "Word," the "Amen," the "Comforter," or "AUM." This sound has been experienced by saints, sages, and mystics throughout recorded history and has been a central part of their spiritual practice and experience of God. It is referred to in the Old and New Testaments of The Bible, the Vedas of India, Buddhist texts, and Sufi literature.

A book talking about such a universal spiritual experience would be compelling in itself. Who doesn't enjoy reading about the experiences of the great saints? But, if it were only about that it would leave us, the readers, sitting on the sidelines. This book also shows you how to attain this high state of consciousness yourself. It is filled with techniques, exercises, and visualizations.

Nayaswami Bharat is also a master storyteller. You will find many inspiring and entertaining examples from the lives of the great saints and guides. Meditation, especially the practice of the AUM technique, confers deep peace, calmness, and a sense of union with creation. I was once with Nayaswami Bharat when he began calling birds to himself. He sat quietly making an odd "pssh, pssh" sound. Soon curious birds began to gather in the branches around him. That was interesting enough, but what I found more fascinating was the fact that the birds showed no fear or shyness in his presence. It was as if they recognized an old friend. You, too, will find an old friend guiding you as you read this book.

—**Nayaswami Jyotish,** *Spiritual Director,*
*Ananda Sangha Worldwide*

# The Melody of Love

*Seek the sound that never ceases.*

RUMI

# The Universal Path to Spirit

AUM is God's consciousness vibrating throughout creation. It is the bridge that unites Nature and Spirit, human and cosmic consciousness. Holy AUM is the stream of God's consciousness into which the soul merges to discover its own highest nature.

There are many ways to enter this stream, many paths and techniques; but once one is in the stream of AUM, his experience is universal: knowledge of the Self, knowledge of the Divine within.

No one path defines or confines the experience. Although one naturally reveres his own path, he shouldn't mistake the path for the goal, lest he separate himself from others on different, yet equally valid, paths.

We are all children of AUM. In Swami Kriyananda's words, "AUM *is*, essentially, what religion is all about. AUM transcends the conflicting ways of belief, and offers mankind a universal highway of awakening."

CHAPTER ONE

## *The Melody of Love*

A loving consciousness pervades this world. From early childhood, I've tried to feel the joy that animates nature. One day while hiking through a remote mountain canyon in California, I could sense the flowers, stones, and cascading stream all laughing and joyfully singing. Every blade of grass, every tiny waterfall and mossy rock, seemed an expression of universal joy—each one blissfully proclaiming this joy to the world.

I sat beside a small, snow-fed pool, delighting in the joy around me. Soon, a robust, cheery little bird came within a few yards of me and began singing. His clear, melodious voice echoed superbly against the surrounding rock walls. The bird's vibrant song and its resounding echo greatly amplified the joy I felt that day on the mountain.

It was only after beginning to study yoga that I discovered that the source of this joy was AUM or Cosmic Sound. Gaelic tradition, too, has it that creation is *The Great Song* sung into existence by the Divine Spirit.

Paramhansa Yogananda once asked God, "Why did you create us?" and He replied, "I did so because I wanted to share My joy." AUM, or the Holy Spirit (Holy Ghost), is the vibration of God's thought; it is Divine Intelligence *in creation*. Yogananda once asked his students, "How could electrons and atoms become water and earth and ether and planets unless there was intelligence guiding them?"

Two sociologists from Baylor University recently asked Americans to describe their view of God. Seventy-three percent of Americans surveyed felt God to be authoritative, critical, or distant. Only twenty-two percent believed in a benevolent Deity. Most imagined a God eager to punish those who err, or a God totally indifferent to His creation.

How one defines God, however, tells more about the one doing the defining than it does about God.

## A LOVING, BENEVOLENT SPIRIT

The teaching of AUM fully unites Spirit with creation. God is AUM, and God BECAME His creation through AUM. Every atom, every living creature is made of the Cosmic Vibration. AUM is the music of all atoms.

Just as striking a gong sends sound ringing through surrounding space, Divine Spirit constantly emanates vibratory AUM to manifest and sustain the universe.* Every atom and cell rings with the vibration of AUM.

Yogananda tells us that God's nature is bliss—that to share His joy He created the universe through Cosmic Vibration. AUM not only proceeds from God, it *is* God. He can be perceived directly by the soul absorbed in listening to the Cosmic Sound. When one communes with AUM, he enters into the stream of God's love and knows for a certainty that the Divine Spirit is lovingly present in this world.

AUM, the Holy Spirit, is called the Comforter, because it gives supreme comfort to the soul. When one is absorbed in AUM, he feels a wonderful peace and harmony. Communion with AUM brings all understanding and marvelous intuitions; it draws right experiences and true friends, even from a distance. No harm can come to one who is in the consciousness of AUM. How could harm come to one who is united with the Essence of the universe?

When one hears the Cosmic Sound, he knows that he could listen to it through all eternity, because AUM is the vibration of

* In *The Promise of Immortality*, Swami Kriyananda writes, "The mind cannot but ask: How can vibrations produce anything as solid as a rock? The answer is that rapid vibrations often give the illusion of having substance. The band of movement created by the tines of a tuning fork may appear solid, if their vibration is broad enough. The blades of a propeller or of an electric fan, similarly, though distinct and separate when they are at rest, appear as a solid wheel when they rotate rapidly."

his very being. After hearing AUM, Saint Francis of Assisi described it as "music so sweet and so beautiful that, had it lasted a moment longer, I would have melted away from the sheer joy of it."

I still remember, after nearly four decades, the joy, reverence, and encouragement to others in Swami Kriyananda's voice as he spoke of the Cosmic Vibration: "Listening to AUM, you'll find the greatest bliss imaginable. It is the loveliest sound in the universe and it thrills you to your heart."

CHAPTER TWO

# The Pristine Vibration

magine you are holding a wooden ball in the palm your hand. A piece of string is tied to the ball and to your middle finger. Gaze at the wooden ball. The stillness of the ball represents motionlessness Spirit.

Now, drop the ball, holding it by the string on your middle finger. Observe how the ball swings gently back and forth. The ball's tiny swings represent the primordial AUM vibration. At the very center of each swing lies unmoving Spirit.

Place your free hand on the ball and bring the ball as far to the left as the string allows. Now release the ball and observe where it goes. It travels in the opposite direction, doesn't it?

"To every action," declares Newton's Third Law of Motion, "there is an equal and contrary reaction." Yoga expresses the same principle as the law of duality or polarity.

Observe how long it takes the ball to stop moving. The pendulums on some of the best clocks can swing freely over a million times.

The calmer the ball becomes, the closer it is to Spirit.

Life's highest goal is "to rise above the duality of creation and perceive the unity of the Creator. Those who cling to [matter consciousness] must accept its essential law of polarity: flow and ebb, rise and fall, day and night, pleasure and pain, good and evil, birth and death." (PARAMHANSA YOGANANDA)

The Ocean of Spirit created the waves that cause the appearance of individuality. The Divine Vibration, however, is not responsible for the behavior of the waves. "The 'Word' itself is not responsible for evil," says Swami Kriyananda, but "only for setting vibration into motion." That motion is, itself, benign. Had only ripples continued to exist, the universe would have remained harmonious, serene, and beautiful. All beings would have lived in harmony with God's will.

Of their own free will, however, souls chose to excite themselves by responding to the wind of *maya,* or delusion, allowing it to whip them to greater and greater excitement. Evil is the conscious impulse toward increasing motion. In *The Promise of Immortality,* Swami Kriyananda writes, "Cosmic delusion is first set in motion by the Spirit. This pristine power is AUM. After that manifestation every ripple has free will to cooperate with the outward-impelling 'wind' of maya, or with the inward pull toward divine union with God."

Without the Cosmic Vibration we would not have the self-awareness necessary to experience God's bliss. Every soul has the choice: to merge with the inward-flowing AUM and live in eternal joy, or to go with the outward-flowing AUM and live far from its divine nature.

## RETURNING TO SPIRIT

To find your way back to God, you have to return the way you came. "Thousands make pilgrimages to the source of the Ganges and other sacred rivers. Such pilgrimages are externalizations of the pilgrimage of the spirit that is accomplished by tracing the inner river of AUM back to its Source." (SWAMI NIR-MALANANDA GIRI) "By following the trail of AUM, you attain Brahma." (SRI RAMAKRISHNA)

Like a prodigal child, one has to return to his home in AUM. There are many byways of belief, but there is only one highway every soul must walk if it is to find God: It must reunite and baptize itself in the original Cosmic Vibration.

"I want to get this matter completely settled into your consciousness, that while prayer and meditation are good, and we should practice, we must not forget that the purpose of meditation is to receive this Holy Ghost. No one, if he doesn't know the

AUM vibration, can get there. That is all there is to it." (PARAM-
HANSA YOGANANDA)

AUM is God's consciousness in creation; its vibratory sound emanates from all atoms. "The meditating yogi first hears the sound of AUM in his right ear. As he deepens his experience of it, he comes to hear it in his whole body as the entire body vibrates with that sound. Thus, feeling AUM throughout the body, he loses identification with self-consciousness as being centered in the medulla, the seat of egoic awareness, and gradually expands with the AUM sound until he is identified with it in all creation." (SWAMI KRIYANANDA)

Once AUM breaks the boundaries of the body there is nothing to stop it. AUM spreads out into infinity, and your consciousness expands with it. When you merge with AUM, you acquire its quality of omnipresence. This state is known as AUM samadhi.

"Through the actual hearing of this Cosmic Vibration, a conscious contact with God or Christ Consciousness can be established. Hence, in order to scientifically contact God, one must reach Him first through AUM." (PARAMHANSA YOGANANDA)

Saints in all religions revere the Cosmic Vibration. "The Qur'an refers to this sound in the words, 'Be! And all became.' Moses heard this very sound on Mount Sinai, when in communion with God; and the same word was audible to Christ when absorbed in his heavenly Father in the wilderness. Shiva heard [AUM] during his Samadhi in . . . the Himalayas. This sound is the source of all revelation to the masters. . . . It is because of this that they know and teach one and the same truth." (HAZRAT INAYAT KHAN, *The Music of Life*)

All spiritual effort and practice eventually brings one to AUM. Every attempt to center your energy calms the outward flowing waves or momentum of your life. For example, while mentally watching your breath, concentrate on the stillness at the center of the breathing process. Swami Kriyananda reminds us to be "aware of the eternal stillness . . . at the center of this gentle movement, until the pauses, like a pendulum slowly coming to rest, are united in breathlessness. . . . The twofold mantra of Hong and Sau combine ultimately in the single vibration of AUM."

## THE GARDEN OF BLISS

The following story is about you
and everyone who was created by God.
It's the story of your very own soul.

See before you
the Heavenly Father, our Creator.
Gaze into His radiant face,
brighter than a thousand suns.

He is a God of joy
and His nature is bliss.
But, as Spirit beyond creation,
He had no one with whom to share His joy.
So God made you.

To enjoy Himself through many,
God projected His consciousness outwards
to manifest the vast universe
through the Sacred AUM Vibration.

AUM is the outpouring of God's love
flowing to you—and to all creation.
When you commune with AUM,
you enter into, and flow with,
the stream of God's love.

Visualize yourself standing with the Heavenly Father.
It is the morning of creation.
Feel the vibrations of His love
entering your heart and filling you with joy.
Dwelling in Cosmic AUM, you live in the paradise
of your Father's Peace, Bliss, and Light.

# CHAPTER THREE

# Blessed Is the Man that Heareth Me

As I was having dinner with a Unitarian minister, after giving a meditation class at his church, he looked at me intently and shared the following experience: "I was going through a very challenging time in my life. Every night I prayed deeply that harmony would prevail, but the situation remained inharmonious and divisive. One night, I suddenly heard the most marvelous sound. It was like a great, rushing wind. I can never forget it. In that moment I felt great reassurance, and I absolutely knew that everything would work out for the best—and it did." He looked at me and said, "What was that sound?"

I was thrilled by the blessing he had received. I told him, "You heard the Holy Spirit—what Jesus called 'the Comforter.'" The AUM vibration had brought into this minister's life the very comfort and healing Jesus described in the Bible.

Another friend of mine had an enthralling experience, also unsought, with AUM. He had come to our Ananda Center on the Peninsula for the first time. That evening, throughout the class, he heard beautiful harp music. He assumed someone in the building was an extremely accomplished musician. But, inexplicably, he continued to hear the melody as he drove home and throughout his week at work.

When he came to class the following week, he said, "I love music, and I have never heard anything so beautiful as that harp music. What is this?"

I said, "You are hearing the sound of AUM manifesting through the third chakra. The sound of the third chakra is like that of a harp. It is because of this lovely sound that people envision angels playing harps in heaven."

## HOW TO HEAR
## THE COSMIC SOUND

AUM is ever present and singing in the silence of your soul. How can you hear its entrancing music? In the following excerpts from Swami Kriyananda's writings, he explains how:

The Cosmic Vibration is inaudible to the human ear, but can be heard inwardly by the "ear" of intuition. People sometimes get a hint of it in places where there is complete silence. They may hear a soft hum, or a gentle murmur like the whisper of wind in the trees. The sound emerges from no discernible point in space, but seems rather to come from everywhere. Patanjali, a great master in ancient India, compared this sound to "oil flowing smoothly out of a barrel." What is heard in quiet surroundings is not so much a spiritually uplifting experience as simply a whisper—like that of a waterfall from afar—of the mighty thunder of AUM perceived in deep meditation.

The harmonious stimulation of each center or chakra is accompanied (albeit not invariably) by subtle sounds. With the stimulation of the coccyx center, the sound of a bumblebee is heard; of the sacral, the sound of a flute; of the lumbar, that of a stringed musical instrument being plucked; of the heart, or dorsal, that of a deep bell; and of the cervical, the sound of wind, or of rushing waters. Heard less perfectly, some of these sounds have the following variations: The bumblebee (with the stimulation of the coccyx center) may sound like a motor; the flute, like crickets, or like trickling water; the bell, high-toned instead of like a deep gong.

Listen intently in the right ear, especially, to any subtle sound you hear. If you hear them in the left ear, try to bring that perception gradually to the right ear. It is not likely that you will hear AUM clearly at first, but concentration on any internal sound will help you gradually to attune your consciousness to the subtle Cosmic Vibration.

Closing the tragi of the ears with the thumbs (the elbows resting lightly on a crosspiece of wood), AUM is chanted mentally at the point between the eyebrows while the mind concentrates on the sounds appearing in the right ear. One should concentrate on only one sound at a time. The very concentration on that sound will attune one to subtler levels of sound, until one hears the Cosmic Vibration. This yoga technique should be learned personally in its various ramifications from a true teacher. It is an important part of the path taught by Paramhansa Yogananda.

Cosmic Vibration is a manifestation of divine consciousness. It manifests not only as sound, but as every other aspect of Divine Vibration. It manifests also as light, divine love, ecstatic bliss, absolute power, heavenly peace, as a vast and dynamic calmness, and as perfect wisdom. All that the mind can know of inspiration derives from that vibration.

The most compelling aspect of the Cosmic Vibration, because the most steady in its manifestation, is sound. This is the aspect, therefore, that is especially emphasized for those who meditate deeply.

THE POWER OF LISTENING

Jobs were scarce during the worldwide depression in the 1930s. In a small Midwest town in the United States the telegraph office announced they'd be hiring a new telegraph operator. On the day of the interview, sixty hopeful men packed the waiting room. To relieve their tension, most of the job applicants joked and chattered loudly with one another. One man, however, sat quietly alone near the office door.

Suddenly the quiet man stood up and walked into the office. A few minutes later, the office manager came to the door and announced, "Thank you all for coming today. We have hired someone for the job."

Why *was* the quiet man hired?

While the other men were talking, the office manager had tapped out in Morse code, "If you hear this message, come in and accept the job." Only one man was calm enough to hear the message.

Paramhansa Yogananda was once asked why his most advanced disciple, Rajarshi Janakananda, progressed so quickly on the spiritual path. Yogananda replied, "He knows how to listen." Just as the quiet man was the only one to hear the telegraph message, the devotee who deeply listens is the one who hears Cosmic AUM.

ॐ

# LISTENING TO LOVE

Visualize the Lord of the Universe standing some distance away. He is continuously speaking to you—sharing His bliss through Cosmic Vibrations of His love. But you cannot hear Him.

Open your divine, inner ear. Listen to the Blessed One.

As you do so, His voice and His love become stronger and more entrancing.

Waves of AUM vibrate within and all around you, everywhere; AUM thrills you with bliss.

# CHAPTER FOUR

# Listening with Devotion

T he sunbathing man, who sits in the sun but doesn't consciously absorb its rays, receives some solar benefit. But the man who consciously soaks in the sun's rays benefits a hundred times more. One should be like the awake sunbather, and dynamically receive the soul-thrilling vibrations of AUM. AUM is not a mere sound heard inside the right ear. It is an omnipresent consciousness, God's tangible presence in creation. One's ability to hear AUM will be determined by the intensity of his mental effort, duration of practice, and love.

When meditating on AUM, first internalize your consciousness, and then listen intently to the loudest, most attractive sound you hear. Feel in this sound the consciousness of AUM. Don't be satisfied with merely hearing the inner sound, but open your heart completely to it. Let your consciousness expand with the Sacred Vibration and feel it dissolve all your attachments and self-definitions. AUM is the Witness: when you commune with AUM you witness a Great Reality and realize that you are a part of that reality.

One saint said that every bird and animal is singing AUM. How could this not be so when everything is a child of Cosmic AUM? While meditating on AUM, treat every sound you hear with reverence. AUM is the inward-pulling call of Divine Mother drawing all Her children back to Her Beloved Presence. In every sound you hear, feel She is conversing with you and calling you to come home to Infinity.

The Mother, a great disciple of Sri Aurobindo, tells of going into her garden to pick vegetables and mentally hearing some of the plants say, "Take me . . . take me," while others stated resolutely, "Don't take me . . . don't take me!" When meditating on AUM, each time the mind wanders in self-involvement, one is like the plant that said, "Don't take me, Mother. I'm busy right now."

"The mind in meditation must be so perfectly still that not a ripple of thought enters it. God, the Subtlest Reality, cannot be perceived except in utter silence." (SWAMI KRIYANANDA) Except for unmoving Spirit, AUM is the subtlest of all realities and can only be perceived by a pure and attentive heart.

One should practice his meditation techniques with a sense of privilege. As you mentally chant and listen to AUM, do so with deep feeling for, and awareness of, its omnipotence and omnipresence.

Concentration on the physical sounds of the body will gradually sensitize you to the subtler astral sounds. Feel that the inner sound is an emissary from Divine Mother. When you receive an emissary from the emperor, the emissary should be treated with the same respect due the emperor himself. Honoring AUM in every sound helps you listen with greater intensity and love.

Many years ago I had a dream that vividly taught me that it is God's power—not one's efforts in meditation—that actually transforms the meditator:

As I was riding a bicycle on a country road surrounded by wheat fields, a large falcon swooped out of the sky and began flying right beside me.

I looked at the falcon and the falcon looked at me—and then smiled. The falcon had a magical presence. When it began flying faster, I pedaled harder to keep up with this magnificent being.

The falcon smiled again, this time seeming to ask, "Can you go faster?" By pedaling furiously, I was barely able to keep up with its faster pace. It took everything I had to stay even with the falcon.

Seeing that I was still keeping up with him, the falcon dramatically increased his speed. To my surprise, I felt a force propelling me forward, and I was able to stay abreast of the rapidly flying falcon.

I wasn't pedaling anymore; I was being carried along by the falcon's presence.

Then the bird flew upward into the sky, and I found myself rising skyward with my falcon friend.

There is a powerful, divine magnetism in the inner sounds that can carry us into the skies of Spirit. Our job is lovingly and energetically to offer ourselves to the Sacred Cosmic Vibration and let it transform us.

The following words by Swami Kriyananda express the profound and encouraging truth on how one really advances spiritually:

You may think, "I can never love God the way the great saints love Him. I'll never have their fervor or joy." But you will find that as you keep reaching for God, He will uplift you. He will give you the power to find Him. You can't generate that power yourself. But your love can draw that power to you.

Visualize before you a very young child reaching up with outstretched arms. Feel his childlike faith and conviction that you will pick him up.

His innocence and trust is irresistible. Feel your heart responding to the child's beautiful innocence. Reach down and lovingly lift him up to you.

God Himself has given you the ability to love. He will respond when you offer yourself to Him with childlike love and trusting expectation. Then, He will reach down and lift you up into His Beloved Presence.

Paramhansa Yogananda said the consciousness and life-force become interiorized when you are inwardly with God. Ultimately it will be your constant, moment-to-moment attunement with God that will someday attract His grace and holy presence as Cosmic Sound and Light.

MEDITATION

## THE SKY AND EARTH
## TOUCHED ME

Prairie grasses swaying in the wind . . . clouds drifting in the sky . . . songbirds flocking in a nearby tree . . . all make the heart sing. We aren't merely observers of nature's beauties. The soul is omnipresent, and everything happens *within* us.

The ego is the soul identified with the body. Egoic consciousness makes one self-absorbed and oblivious of other realities. When one is immersed in nature, the "body vanishes and the freed soul goes abroad." (JOHN MUIR) Only by expanding beyond the physical body can one commune with God.

People enjoy being in nature because there they see ennobling qualities they want for themselves. In its myriad forms, nature helps enrich and expand the soul. Sri Ramakrishna asked his disciple Master Mahasaya to meditate whenever he saw an expanse of water, because the placidity of water reminds one of the vastness of God.

Richard Jefferies, the English poet, spoke of everything in nature—a flower, a lake—as "touching him and giving him something of itself." He "spoke to the sea . . . and desired its strength." He addressed the sun, and consciously drew upon the soul equivalent of its light. He looked at the sky, gazed into its depths, and felt the "blue sky drawing his soul toward it, and there it rested."

Feeling nature's essence within your body and all around you helps you feel God's body. The best way to feel nature within you, Swami Kriyananda says, is to relate from your center (in the spine) to the center of everything you observe. When you see a striking rock or tree, commune with its spiritual essence; feel it becoming alive in you.

In India there was a hermit who had an unusual way of praying. While the other hermits recited the scriptures, repeated mantras, or practiced breathing exercises, this "atypical" hermit expressed his devotion differently. After coming out of his cave, he'd greet the morning sun, enjoy the sunlight on the Ganges, and listen to the birds. Every time he saw something that delighted him, he'd joyfully clap his hands in approval and exclaim, "Well done, Lord! Well done!"

"All life leaps like a dancer when gazing I see only Thee." (SWAMI KRIYANANDA) When the consciousness expands and all nature becomes one's body, one feels oneself moving in, and delighting in, everything.

May you, like that hermit, see and delight in God everywhere.

## THE SKY AND EARTH
## TOUCHED ME

Go to a beautiful natural area that feels vibrantly alive, such as a small stream lined with maple trees, a flowery mountain meadow, or an aspen forest. (One can also do this exercise indoors while looking out a window.)

Ask Divine Mother to reveal Herself to you through all Her forms and appearances: the flying birds . . . flowering trees . . . and distant ridges.

When something captivates you, relate from your center to its center. Commune with its spiritual essence, feel it becoming alive in you.

Feel that aspect of nature awakening equivalent soul qualities inside you. For example, a towering mountain may inspire feelings of soul aspiration.

Lovingly look at what has captivated you, and mentally include its name in the following sentence: *The _____ touched me . . . and gave me part of itself.* For example, if you observe a raven soaring high in the sky, say, "The <u>raven</u> touched me . . . and gave me part of itself."

Continue to practice as you sit or walk, saying, "the _____ touched me," or "Divine Mother touched me."

Be aware of the inner lift of pleasure the sight gives you, and share that feeling with God.

One day, when Jesus was surrounded by a jostling crowd, a sick woman of great faith quietly and lovingly reached out and touched his robe. Because of her devotion, she was instantly healed. Jesus asked his disciples, "Who touched me?" Though many people were touching Jesus, only that woman touched him with the kind of love that drew his spiritual blessings.

Most people, John Muir said, are like little marbles, rigidly alone, "having no conscious sympathy or relationship to anything." God, however, has surrounded each soul with other people and with nature's beauties to help him expand his consciousness and self-identity. The more you commune with the divine in nature, the more you'll feel the joy of the universe passing through you.

CHAPTER FIVE

# Chanting and Attuning to AUM

here is tremendous power in chanting the syllable AUM. "When you utter 'AUM,' it travels not only all around the earth, but throughout all space and eternity." (PARAMHANSA YOGANANDA) "AUM is not a word, but God Himself." (SWAMI VIVEKANANDA)

Why do we say AUM or Amen at the end of every prayer? We want our words to be accepted into the truth of Cosmic AUM. Swami Rama Tirtha said AUM is the point at which speech and thought stop and the soul melts into divinity. Prayers "spoken in the vibrant consciousness of the Divine Sound, will not only be heard by God, but will be energized and filled with His infinite power." (SWAMI KRIYANANDA)

The purpose of chanting AUM is to attune to its divine consciousness. To be successful, one must chant AUM with love, conviction, and intuition. The words from Swami Kriyananda's song "Cloisters", "Offered candles in prayer to your Light," beautifully describe the devotee's offering his chant of AUM to the all-pervading Cosmic Vibration.

Sound is associated with the ether element, the most spiritually refined element, located at the cervical (or throat) chakra. (The other elements are air, fire, water, and earth—in descending order of manifestation.) Only a thin veil separates the ether element from pure Consciousness; only ether is in direct contact with Spirit. The nature of the ether element explains why the Cosmic Sound and music have tremendous magnetism to influence us.

Hearing is the only sense that has two faculties: active and passive. One can both hear and generate sound; no other sense can do this. For example, the sense of smell cannot generate smells. When one chants the syllable AUM aloud or mentally, he is using hearing's active power to generate the actual sound of AUM as closely as he can. Every time one chants AUM, he should lovingly try to replicate the reality of AUM.

Feel that AUM is coming from your soul, and harmonize your consciousness with it. As you become more interiorized, you will no longer be merely repeating the syllable of AUM and affirming its reality; you will hear and feel the Cosmic Vibration singing within and all around you, and you will be intoxicated with the bliss of the "music of the spheres."

# CHAPTER SIX

# Expand Your Consciousness

"AUM is the ladder which takes the aspirant to the loftiest levels of Superconsciousness." (SWAMI SIVANANDA) The Mundaka Upanishad proclaims AUM to be the bow, the arrow to be the soul, and the target, Brahma, or Cosmic Spirit. AUM is the Omnipotent Force that propels each soul toward God.

Swami Kriyananda describes below how the power and magnetism inherent in the Cosmic Vibration uplift our consciousness:

> As you hear the inner sounds, you begin to concentrate more and more deeply. By concentrating on these sounds you'll gradually trace them back to their source in AUM. As you listen more deeply you'll find your body

dissolving in the great sound of AUM; then, expanding beyond the body, you'll find this AUM sound gradually engulfing the world around you. You'll know you *are* that sound, and it will expand out beyond infinity. And you'll find yourself at one with all creation.

When we ring a gong, the sound travels outward in all directions. In the same way, our consciousness expands with the Cosmic Sound. Once we experience AUM beyond the body, there is nothing to prevent our consciousness from expanding with the Cosmic Vibration to infinity.

Just as one million cubic feet of air can be compressed into one cubic foot, so is cosmic consciousness compressed by egoic consciousness. When the soul identifies with the body, it confines its awareness of Cosmic Consciousness to a tiny portion of matter. (Thus saints say that devotees must give up their attachments in order to free themselves for omnipresent consciousness.)

When compressed air escapes its container, it rapidly spreads to fill the surrounding space. One's consciousness expands similarly when it breaks free of body-attachment. Once AUM is heard throughout the body and the entire body vibrates with the Cosmic Sound, one transcends self-consciousness, which is centered in the medulla oblongata at the base of the brain. One then gradually expands with AUM until he identifies with all creation.

Sacred AUM wants to liberate your consciousness.

Listen to it so deeply that you become lost in the inner sounds. Don't be satisfied with only listening, but increase your consciousness in AUM. Feel or visualize yourself expanding to the boundaries of eternity with Cosmic, All-Spreading AUM.

## VISUALIZATIONS

Visualizations are statements of truth that awaken the soul's memory of its deeper reality. After you've finished your meditation techniques, when your consciousness is uplifted, visualizations can sensitively guide you to deeper experiences of divine realities.

Paramhansa Yogananda has written the *All-Spreading AUM Meditation* (see below) to help us not only hear the cosmic sound but also *feel* its actual presence in every unit of space. Then, taking us further, Yogananda attunes us to the still, watchful state beyond vibratory creation.

At the heart of every vibrating atom lies the stillness of God. In his book, *The Promise of Immortality*, Swami Kriyananda explains that the "Cosmic Vibration would be incomplete without the stillness of Spirit subtly reflected at the center of all movement. In order for cosmic creation to be truly vibratory, and not helter-skelter movement in all directions, it needs to be centered, not at some point in outer space, but at the heart of every vibration. From that center, movement begins. AUM is an emanation of Spirit, and reflects at its own center Spirit's motionless consciousness."

Use the following meditation to cultivate a greater feeling of AUM vibrating beyond your body. Try, also, to sense underlying the AUM vibration, the vibrationless calm of unmoving Spirit.

EXERCISE

# THE ALL-SPREADING
# AUM MEDITATION

*~ Based on Paramhansa Yogananda's Occult Vision meditation ~*

Close your eyes. Relax your body . . . and mind.

Concentrate on the ball of darkness that surrounds you. Feel this ball. Then imagine or feel it filled with the vibrations of AUM.

Imagine the ball of darkness and vibration becoming as big as the earth. Then expand the ball of vibration to the distant stars, galaxies, and all space. Feel and hear AUM emanating from every atom in creation.

Fill this infinite ball of vibration with the consciousness of Bliss, unceasing watchfulness (with attention equally concentrated everywhere), the consciousness of immortality, knowledge, peace, and all-pervading energy and life energy.

Remain identified with this highest awareness, as long as you can—as often as you can. Then God will be real to you, and you will find His conscious guidance in everything.

CHAPTER SEVEN

# Absolute Security
# and Assurance

Communing with AUM makes one fearless. One's reality shifts from the ego, which can never be secure, to the Cosmic Vibration, which is the essence of all creation. Ego consciousness isolates us from the rest of life. Those who deeply merge with AUM, however, know and say, "I am the whole universe. What can possibly harm me?"

In his book *Rays of the One Light*, Swami Kriyananda writes, "Human vision beholds individuality and separation everywhere. Divine vision beholds the oneness of cosmic vibration, of which all things, no matter how diverse, are manifestations. Cosmic Sound and Cosmic Light: These are eternal. The world, as revealed to us by our senses, is illusory."

When one is deeply absorbed in AUM and feels its awesome power, the external world is seen as only a dream-thought. One knows, without a doubt, that only AUM is real.

Swami Rama Tirtha said blissfully, "Nature is my body," because through deep communion with AUM he felt he was *united* with the trees and farthest stars. In his chant, "Marching Light," he expresses the omnipotent confidence native to every soul who knows AUM:

> The world turns aside to make room for me;
> I come, Blazing Light! And the shadows must flee.
> I ride on the Tempests, astride on the Gale,
> My gun is the Lightning my shots never fail.
> I hitch to my chariot the Fates and the Gods.
> With Thunder of cannon proclaim it abroad:
> Wake! Wake up! Be free,
> Liberty! Liberty! Liberty! AUM

The Cosmic Vibration is beyond duality; therefore, in its reality, there's no opposite or opposition. In its consciousness, there is no myself *against* another—but myself *as* all others.

Swami Sivananda illustrated the universal consciousness of one immersed in AUM with the analogy of a canvas with material objects painted on it: "The canvas is real, but the pictures in the canvas are unreal because the fire [painted] in the canvas cannot burn your fingers, the knife in the canvas cannot cut your fingers, the tiger in the canvas cannot bite you. AUM is the only solid reality."

Swami Kriyananda has written a marvelous visualization for affirming and experiencing the universal consciousness of AUM. You can use this visualization when you feel in opposition to anything or anyone, or to unite with AUM during meditation.

> Imagine a choir composed of every atom in the universe, each one an individual, but all of them singing together in blissful harmony.
>
> In your own mind, join that mighty choir, composed of all life. Determine from today on to sing in harmony with the universe. Don't impose on the great anthem of life your little wishes for how you want the music to sound. Unite your notes to that Infinite Sound.
>
> The more you do so, the more deeply you will know yourself to be an expression of the soaring anthem of Infinity.
>
> —from *Awaken to Superconsciousness*

### NOTHING CAN TOUCH YOU

"When AUM came," a lady once said to Paramhansa Yogananda, "all my troubles vanished." My friend, Mari, told me recently how her troubles had also vanished when she attuned to the consciousness of AUM.

Several years ago she was waiting to make a deposit at her bank when, suddenly, she found herself in the middle of a robbery. It was a highly stressful situation, and Mari said she "lost it" emotionally.

After the robbery, Mari was disappointed in herself for reacting so emotionally. To change this tendency in herself, she began chanting AUM all day long. Whenever there was a tense situation, Mari would silently and lovingly call on the healing power of AUM to calm herself and others.

AUM is the Great Comforter. Paramhansa Yogananda said that when you are in the consciousness of AUM, nothing can touch you.

Three years later, Mari was again at her bank when another robbery occurred. This time it was a much more violent one.

During this bank heist, Mari was knocked to the floor. But her long practice of thinking of and chanting AUM kept her calm and centered.

As Mari began crawling discreetly away from the robbers, a hysterical woman latched on to her; Mari guided the terrified woman out of the robbers' sight, where they both would be safe.

Later, during an interview with the FBI, Mari was told that the odds of being involved in two bank robberies were incredibly low. She was the only witness who could give an accurate description of the robbers. Mari attributed this ability to the calmness she felt from tuning in to the unifying presence of AUM.

While backpacking in California's Southern Sierra Nevada Mountains, three women from Ananda Village had a dramatic experience of the power of AUM. On the fourth day of their trip, a furious thunderstorm caught them at ten thousand feet. Loud cracks of lightning and massive explosions of thunder crashed around them. Torrential rain fell; then hail began to fall harder and harder. Desperate for shelter, they ran to a couple of small trees, which soon proved inadequate protection against the pounding hailstorm.

Seeing a large tree nearby, they bolted for its sheltering branches. Already wet, they struggled out of their packs and dug for their rain jackets. The temperature, meanwhile, had plummeted, and the hail began to fall even harder.

They knew they were in trouble. In their drenched condition, hypothermia was a real possibility. They badly needed shelter. Yet, standing under the highest tree around wasn't wise—because tall trees are perfect lightning rods. They wondered aloud, "Do we risk hypothermia or lightning strikes?" Both options were dangerous.

Then one of the women began chanting to all-pervading AUM. The two other ladies quickly joined in. Suddenly, they felt as if a bubble of protection surrounded them. Their fear was gone—a feeling of awe and gratitude filled their hearts. For twenty minutes, they chanted and enjoyed the majestic show of lightning and hail. After the storm, everything was transformed into a white wonderland; they felt blessed beyond measure by the love and protection of AUM.

Being in AUM gives one absolute security. The whole world could go up in flames and it wouldn't matter to you. Swami Rama Tirtha was a great devotee of AUM. He chanted AUM always—during lectures, conversations, and solitary walks in nature. Before he knew AUM, he said, every whiff of wind threw him off balance. But after constant practice and remembrance of AUM, he became completely free of annoyance, anxiety, and fear. He told his students, "If one man can do this, you can, too."

## HEALING TECHNIQUES
### WITH AUM

If you are troubled before going to sleep, write AUM or Amen on your pillow with your fingers. Mentally visualize light around your body, look into the spiritual eye and say several times, mentally or loudly: I am Light. Darkness fly away.

Standing or sitting, touch both of your palms in front of your body, and then swing them to touch behind your back, and then forward again several times in rapid succession, chanting AUM, and you will be protected.

PARAMHANSA YOGANANDA
*Karma and Reincarnation*

# CHAPTER EIGHT

## Your Friend and Liberator

leeping babies smile blissfully, the saints say, because they're listening to AUM. A human mother sings a lullaby to comfort her baby; the Divine Mother sings Her lullaby of love to comfort all creation.

Through AUM, God's grace flows into the world. After first hearing it and discovering its continuous sound, an Ananda student said, "AUM is ever present. All I need to do is remember to listen!"

The Cosmic Vibration is loving, conscious, and responsive. Paramhansa Yogananda spoke of how the sound of AUM would change into the English or Bengali language to give him precise instructions. He said, "You have absolutely no idea of the wonderful realizations and intuitions [listening to AUM] will give you. If you practice it regularly, faithfully, and reverently, you will get them all by and by."

When disciples would ask Paramhansa Yogananda to give them a mantra. Yogananda would suggest, "AUM Guru," explaining that this mantra is a prayer to the guru asking him to introduce the disciple to AUM. "Then," Yogananda would add with a smile, "AUM becomes your teacher."

AUM is the Cosmic Redeemer because it annihilates the mind. The sages of India say that the restless mind is finally trapped by its attraction to AUM and samadhi is achieved. "Just as light is the property of a lighted lamp," Lahiri Mahasaya said, "so the sound of AUM is the intrinsic property of the stage of samadhi."

Just as a child who has been separated from his mother quickly achieves oneness with her when he is again in her presence, so does the devotee become totally absorbed while in AUM. Even wild animals are attracted to the Cosmic Sound. Snakes, deer, and other wild beasts in the forests of the Himalayas have often come to sit peacefully beside a hermit who's chanting AUM. AUM's effect on animals shouldn't be surprising, because everything in creation is, in a very real sense, music or vibration; and Holy AUM, the purest of all melodies, naturally captivates every being.

ॐ

# FOLLOW THE TRAIL OF AUM

When one closes his ears, the external sounds of the world disappear. His consciousness is drawn inward to the sounds of the physical body, then deeper within, to the astral sounds of the chakras. If one continues following the trail of AUM, Ramakrishna says, he will find God.

Read the following visualization and travel the blessed trail that leads to Holy AUM and beyond:

Imagine you are standing in a heavily wooded forest, far from the ocean. Listen to the sounds of the forest all around you.

Very faintly . . . you can also hear a distant roar. You cannot see the ocean and have no idea how far away it is. But you know that where there is a roaring sound, there must be the ocean. With great expectation, follow the sound of the ocean, and listen intently along the way, making sure that the ocean's roar is becoming stronger and stronger in your ears.

You walk for some time, then see dazzling blue sky appearing between the trees on the ridge above you. You must be getting close.

You crest the ridge and hear the mighty rumble of the ocean. Lo, before you, luminous waves are crashing along the shore. The roar of the waves thrills every cell in your being.

Your soul leaps blissfully out of your body and expands to unite with the surf, rocks, and sand. You joyfully delight in, and fly with, the soaring seagulls. You are in everything you see. You are blooming in the flowers, scuttling across the sand, and surging in the waves. Your soul delights in the blissful hum that emanates from every atom in creation.

Sensing that there is still more to experience, you raise your eyes above the crashing waves, and their thunderous roar. Silent Stillness draws you into the vast, blue ocean of Spirit: calm and serene. Like a raindrop splashing on a lake, you melt in the Infinite Sea.

# CHAPTER NINE

# What If I Don't Hear AUM?

**Y**ou can experience AUM without hearing its vibratory sounds, because Divine Spirit has created many vibrations. The first is Cosmic Vibration, which manifests as sound and light. The secondary vibrations are Cosmic Love, Wisdom, Power, Peace, Joy, and Calmness. All religious truths and experiences are centered in Cosmic AUM. When you feel divine inspiration in the form of Cosmic Joy, for example, you *are* experiencing Holy AUM.

"The eight attributes [or vibrations] rarely, if ever, appear all at once. They resemble, rather, the facets of a diamond. Each is presented at the right moment, and to the right person. Meditators usually feel themselves attracted to one attribute or another, and are therefore more likely to experience that attribute in themselves. The higher stages of meditation entail progressively deeper absorption in one attribute or another . . . until the soul expands to become all of them." (SWAMI KRIYANANDA)

People sometimes become discouraged when they don't hear AUM clearly. It's helpful to remember that hearing AUM purely and constantly signifies a deep state of meditation, which, if it is sustained, leads to samadhi. Listening reverently to whatever sounds you hear is the key to deepening your experience of AUM. A friend described once, during meditation, hearing a very soft sound in the background. He assumed it was just a sound made by his physical body. As he focused on it, however, it became the thrilling sound of AUM.

## AUM IS ALWAYS WITH YOU

"Yogananda loved to tell about the musk deer of the Himalayas," wrote Swami Kriyananda. "At a certain season of the year this deer secretes in a pouch in its navel the delightful fragrance of musk. The deer runs frantically about, trying to find the source of this wonderful perfume. O musk deer! a poet once wrote, Why could you not understand that the fragrance you sought was ever with you in your very self?"

In the 1940s, the Yale scientist Harold Burr discovered that during its life cycle a salamander has an etheric field shaped like an adult. The energy body is present even when the amphibian is in the form of an unfertilized egg. This ever-present etheric pattern guides the growth of the baby salamander to full maturity.

We are children of AUM. Jesus told his disciples, "No man hath ascended up to heaven, but he that came down from heaven." Just as a baby salamander is guided by its etheric pattern, so every soul is guided back to infinite AUM.

## SPIRITUAL PRACTICES
## CALM OUR VIBRATION

Cosmic Vibration made and sustains us. The ego, however, magnifies the pristine movement of Cosmic Vibration much as a child on a swing uses his energy to increase the swing's existing movement. Just as the playing child swings in bigger and bigger arcs, so does the ego move away from AUM because of its attraction to outwardness.

Yogananda said, "When motion ceases, God appears." One cannot go immediately from movement-consciousness to stillness. He needs first to attune to the Cosmic Vibration, which then guides him to Christ Consciousness, and beyond.

Stopping desire-created movement and attuning to God's original movement—Cosmic Vibration—is the "one highway every soul must walk." Even if one has never heard the Cosmic Sound, even if he does not know of AUM's existence, his spiritual practices and attitudes—through calming his vibratory movement—will bring him to AUM. Swami Kriyananda says that practicing contentment alone "leads ultimately to the realization of Divine Bliss in every atom of creation," because that soul is no longer seeking fulfillment outside himself.

While in solitary confinement in Communist Romania for his Christian faith, pastor Richard Wurmbrand heard in the silence a sound "more beautiful than the most beautiful music. A sound," he said, "that you never tire of." Holy AUM came to him unsought. In time, the Cosmic Sound will come to you, too, and you'll receive wondrous realizations and bliss from the Blessed Comforter.

Swami Kriyananda said that meditating on AUM is a "slow starter but a strong finisher. In the beginning it requires lots of effort, lots of concentration, lots of will power, and lots of devotion, but bit by bit it won't be work at all. Hearing a little sound in your ear won't mean very much in the beginning. It will be a little boring. I tell you that so you won't give up."

"Do not be impatient. Keep on steadily. Do not mind [God's] silence. Remember, He is listening. As in everything else, the highest results cannot be attained in a day or even in days. I speak from experience—not only my own, but that of centuries of experience by the great yogis in my country. You, too, can have the same glorious experience as they, if you persevere in your practice." (PARAMHANSA YOGANANDA)

If hearing AUM's captivating sounds seems a distant potential, continue your other meditation and devotional practices.

Go deeper and deeper into your experience of God, and keep open to AUM's holy presence. The more your consciousness becomes interiorized, the more easily will you commune with inner, spiritual realities.

It's essential that we meditate with love. Swami Kriyananda gives the following advice for keeping the right attitude during meditation:

> The spiritual path is not about the experiences we receive in meditation, but about the refinement and purity of our self-offering to God. The more we think about how we can get more realization, the more we fall into delusion. Instead it has to be constant giving—in that giving, God can give us more.
>
> To eliminate the strain and tension of trying to concentrate, release also the thought, "I am meditating." Think rather: "The Cosmic Vibration is reaffirming through me, its own reality. Cosmic Love, through me, is yearning for God's love; Cosmic Joy, through me, is rejoicing in our Infinite Beloved."

## YOUR BODY IS THE TEMPLE OF THE HOLY GHOST

In the beginning, says the Bible, God's voice thundered marvelously and moved the "waters." His thought, which vibrates, creates and animates the heavens and earth. God's grace, through Cosmic Vibration, has created you. To declare, "I don't hear AUM, so it must not be for me," is to say, "I am separate from the rest of creation." This separateness simply isn't possible.

Cosmic Sound is the most constant and tangible expression of God. "AUM is a sound with which all can commune, and into which also, in time, all can merge." (SWAMI KRIYANANDA) The day will come when you'll know that AUM is—and always has been—your greatest Friend.

# CHAPTER TEN

# Seeing AUM in Nature

"True communion with nature can be done only inwardly, through communion with AUM." (SWAMI KRIYANANDA) A disciple of Yogananda told me this experience: "While bathing in the river, I cognized AUM as the water swirling around my body, in the solidity of the river rocks, and in the sun's rays on my bare chest. While hearing AUM roaring in the rapids, I felt the waters of Holy AUM coursing through me."

AUM solidifies into matter through different rates of astral vibration. These vibratory currents are the elements of ether, air, fire, water, and earth. In nature we can see solidified expressions of these elements: in the emptiness of space, moving air currents, fiery volcanoes, rippling lakes, and stately mountains.

While in the wilderness, John Muir felt every cell and atom, vibrating with music and life, and the mountains seemingly dissolve into the "incomparable Spirit of Holy Light."

Seeing vibratory AUM in physical forms unites you with the essence of Life. The following exercise helps you feel AUM's presence tangibly in creation and makes AUM more real to your consciousness.

Practice this meditation outdoors in a beautiful garden or natural area.

## SEEING AUM IN NATURE

*"AUM not only proceeds from God, it is God."*
PARAMHANSA YOGANANDA

AUM is Divine Mother existing in the heart of all things. During the *Seeing AUM in Nature* exercise, try to feel Her blissful presence in everything you see and hear.

### THE SUN IS THE FORM OF AUM

Look at the sun. See its rays flowing down, warming the nearby hills and enlivening the trees and flower-covered meadows. Reflect on how all life depends on the sun. Gaze at a plant and feel how it is nourished by the great power emanating from our star.

Just as an iceberg is formed of water, so the sun is formed of AUM. "The sun," Kabir said, "is the most immediate 'physical' form of AUM we can experience, for it is really solidified, materialized AUM."

See the sun as AUM. Think of it as AUM materialized. Feel its vibratory rays descending from heaven and bringing into manifestation and sustaining all life around you.

See each bird and flower as AUM solidified. Behind every form, sense AUM's underlying presence and vibrancy. Feel and hear all nature proclaiming and singing AUM

*"Even in outward, physical imitations, sounds can be thrilling."*

SWAMI KRIYANANDA

Let every sound remind you of AUM. Listen intently to the rushing wind—the roar of a river—the buzzing of a bee—the joyful song of a bird. Commune with each sound you hear. Open yourself completely to it; feel it coming into you. Listen for and feel AUM in every outer sound.

Watch the wind flow through the trees and grassy fields. See in every trembling leaf and sailing cloud—in every movement—Sacred AUM vibrating.

Try to perceive AUM in everything you do, see, and hear. Observe the ways God, through Cosmic AUM, expresses Himself. See how your Invisible Mother, in creation, has become visible.

Notice how each tree, like each person, is marvelously unique. Take delight in the countless expressions of AUM you see before you. Communing with AUM helps one understand and utter the language of all creation. When one unites with AUM, he unites with all existence.

Live in the consciousness of AUM. "You are not a physical body, but a blissful manifestation of AUM." (SWAMI KRIYANANDA) One who constantly sings AUM during his activities, and with his whole being, makes his life a continuous song of joy.

# CHAPTER ELEVEN

# Go Within

AUM is devoid of duality. It's the only sound not made by striking another object, and so it is called the "unstruck" sound. AUM's thrilling sounds cannot be heard by physical ears, but only by the intuitive power of the soul. Below, a devotee describes AUM's pristine quality after hearing it emanate from his heart center:

I heard the sound of church bells and it was utterly beautiful and crystal clear. It had a sense of lightness and clarity unlike anything I have ever experienced. If you can imagine the heaviness of ordinary sound produced by the air it must pass through, this was completely un-like that. It was the essence of sound before it meets air—as if the sound was conveyed on light through space with no grossness whatsoever.

AUM resides at the center of one's being. The Cosmic Vibration created us by descending into the brahmanadi channel, the causal spine. From there, it descends into outward manifestation to create one's astral and physical spines and bodies. To unite with Spirit, one needs to retrace the pathway by which he descended. "The opening of brahmanadi channel is at the top of the head. On reaching this point, the yogi becomes reunited with omnipresence, for the last sheath has been removed that closes him off from Infinity." (SWAMI KRIYANANDA)

Cosmic AUM has tremendous magnetic power to draw one to God. It opens the spiritual channels in the body, pierces the chakras, reverberates in the deep spine, and is the sound of the rising *Kundalini* energy.

Spiritual growth accelerates as the *Kundalini* current rises through the deep spine to the Spiritual Eye. This ascent, however, is usually blocked by the outward flowing energy in the chakras. Hearing the sounds of the chakras means that the life-force is flowing back into the spine. Concentrating on these sounds deepens them, and redirects the currents (that flow through each chakra) back into the spine.

To deepen your experience of AUM, you'll find it beneficial to practice meditation techniques that draw your awareness inward. "Once the mind is interiorized, and withdrawn from its identification with the world and with the body, the inner sounds become all-absorbing." (PARAMHANSA YOGANANDA) AUM's inner sounds are often likened to heavenly music because they carry the one who hears them to higher realms.

When one withdraws his life-force into the spine and brain, he experiences another world—a world of Spirit. One night in Mexico, a friend of mine was standing on a hotel balcony enjoying the city lights spread out before him. Suddenly a power failure plunged the city into darkness. As the lights of the city were darkened, the brilliance of the stars came alive. The glow of the city had overpowered the stars' subtler light. In the same way, focusing on material realities makes one deaf to AUM's mighty roar.

AUM is heard fully when one's awareness is centered in the sixth chakra, or "spiritual eye," located at the point between the eyebrows. Concentrating at this point helps awaken the subtle astral sounds of the chakras. Those who want to commune with AUM will find it extremely beneficial to focus at the spiritual eye during their daily activities and to practice meditation techniques that withdraw the life-force into the spine and brain. "Through the divine eye . . . the yogi sails his consciousness into omnipresence . . . hearing AUM. Long concentration on the liberating spiritual eye has enabled the yogi to destroy all delusions concerning matter." (PARAMHANSA YOGANANDA)

To help devotees commune with AUM and merge their spirits with Infinity, Paramhansa Yogananda brought to the West the sacred path of Kriya Yoga, which consists of four main techniques. Like each leg of a stool, each technique helps to support the others. Each one emphasizes an aspect of inner awakening that is universal for all seekers.

1. **Discovering one *is* energy and not just a physical body.**

   To help one experience himself as energy, Paramhansa Yogananda created a series of physical movements, the *Energization Exercises*. In the process of tensing and relaxing the muscles in order to feel the life-force flowing through the body, the student learns to direct the divine energy within.

2. **Interiorizing and concentrating the awakened energy at the spiritual eye.**

   The *Hong-Sau* Technique is an ancient practice used in various forms by many spiritual traditions. By watching the breath inside the nose—without controlling it—the practitioner becomes increasingly still, relaxed, and uplifted with a growing focus at the spiritual eye.

3. **Expanding the consciousness by feeling AUM vibrating throughout the body, and, then, the universe.**

Yogananda taught a specific method to: close the ears to outside sounds, redirect the energy that normally flows outward to the senses, and attune the practitioner to the subtle sounds of AUM.

## 4. Withdrawing the life-force into the deep astral spine.

The Kriya Yoga technique magnetizes the astral spine by offering the inhaling breath into the outgoing breath, a practice which gradually neutralizes the breath and releases the blissful *Kundalini* current to flow upward to the spiritual eye, where enlightenment occurs. Because Kriya controls the mind directly through the life-force, Paramhansa Yogananda described the technique as "the easiest, most effective, and most scientific avenue of approach to the Infinite. It is through Kriya that the devotee reaches the Kingdom of Heaven within his body and listens to the celestial music." Kriya Yoga, he said, was the fulfillment of Jesus Christ's promise to send the Comforter.

- You can read more about the path of Kriya Yoga in Paramhansa Yogananda's *Autobiography of a Yogi,* at www.ananda.org.

- You can learn more about withdrawing the life-force, and the *Hong-Sau* technique, in the supplementary *Daily Meditator* articles at the end of this book: "The Joy of Interiorization" and "Why Hong-Sau Works."

- If you are new to meditation, or haven't yet used a technique to interiorize your energy, the *Hong-Sau* technique can be invaluable to your practice. It's one of the most ancient of all yoga practices; Paramhansa Yogananda called it, "the greatest contribution of India's spiritual science to the world." He said to practice "the technique calmly, with relaxation—even with reverence—and feel in that calmness that you are placing yourself in readiness to listen to, and to become absorbed in, the Cosmic Vibration, AUM. *Hong-Sau* will help to put you in contact with the Great Spirit, who is present in you as your soul, and whose expression is vibration."

    To learn this technique, you can visit either the *Ananda Meditation Support* website at www.ananda.org/meditation/support/articles/ or *The Gift of Inner Peace* website at www.giftofpeace.org.

The Gift of Inner Peace

five minutes of serenity
www.giftofpeace.org

## THE TUNNEL OF LIGHT

In *Awaken to Superconsciousness*, Swami Kriyananda has written a marvelous visualization for merging into the spiritual eye:

> Concentrate at the point between the eyebrows. Visualize there a tunnel of golden light. Mentally enter that tunnel, and feel yourself surrounded by a glorious sense of happiness and freedom. As you move through the tunnel, feel yourself bathed by the light until all worldly thoughts disappear.
>
> After soaring through the tunnel as long as you feel to do so, visualize before you a curtain of deep, violet-blue light. Pass through that curtain into another tunnel of deep, violet-blue light. Feel the light surrounding

you. Slowly, the tunnel walls disappear in blue light. Expand your consciousness into that light—into infinite freedom and bliss. Now there is no tunnel. There is only the all-encompassing blueness and bliss of infinity.

At last, visualize before you a silvery-white, five-pointed star of light. Mentally spread out your arms and legs, assuming with your body the shape of that star. Give yourself to it in body, mind, and soul as you surrender every thought, every feeling to absolute, Self-existing Bliss.

Bliss cascades gently over you, like a waterfall of mist, filling your heart with ineffable peace.

# CHAPTER TWELVE

# How the Guru Frees Us

esus told his disciples, when the Holy Ghost comes, "ye shall receive power." Later, Jesus "breathed on them and said, 'Receive ye the Holy Ghost.'" The guru sends the Comforter, and through the Comforter, the disciple receives the guru's inner blessings. AUM's expanding power spreads the disciple's consciousness to Infinity; he hears and feels the hum of every atom in the universe. The disciple begins at last, to experience the guru's consciousness.

Mrs. Wellman, an elderly American lady, once came to Swami Rama Tirtha for a private interview. She wept as she recounted her domestic troubles to the swami, who sat cross-legged with his eyes closed. No kind look or word of sympathy came from him. As he continued to sit like a stone statue, Mrs. Wellman silently muttered, "These Indians are so impudent and proud."

Then Swami Rama Tirtha opened his eyes. He looked at Mrs. Wellman and said, "Mother," and chanted his favorite mantra, "AUM, AUM!" His eyes, bursting with power, transmitted to her a strange, new consciousness. "I seemed to have been lifted from the earth," she said. "I swam in the air as a figure of light, and I felt myself the mother of the Universe. My joy never fails me. Oh! The word OM reverberates through my bones."[*]

Paramhansa Yogananda said of his disciple, Sister Gyanamata, "she has lived in my vibrations for a long time." Whenever he sent her a special inner blessing, she would feel it instantly. While living in Seattle, she had several serious physical ailments. When Gyanamata's condition worsened, she wrote a letter to Yogananda, who was then lecturing in New York City, asking for his prayers. On the day she thought the letter had arrived, she heard AUM's tremendous roar and felt her body shaking. Her guru had received her letter and had sent Cosmic AUM to heal her.

Bathing in AUM's sacred vibrations is the true baptism. The technique for listening to AUM is usually given as an initiation because of the importance of the guru's magnetism. The guru is beyond vibratory creation and guides his disciples—through Cosmic Vibration—to the deepest states of enlightenment.

As you listen for, and attune to, the inner sounds, pray to your guru, if you have one. Ask to be introduced to Holy AUM.

A guru once told her disciples, "I'm the gatekeeper. When God is pleased with you, I'll give you AUM."

[*] *The Story of Swami Rama Tirtha*, by Puran Singh.

In *The Essence of Self Realization,* Paramhansa Yogananda shares the stages that unite the devotee with Spirit:

> AUM fills the brain; its vibration moves down the spine, bursting open the door of the heart's feeling, then flowing out into the body. The whole body vibrates with the sound of AUM.
>
> Gradually, with ever-deeper meditation, the consciousness expands with that sound. Moving beyond the confines of the body, it embraces the vastness of infinite vibration. You realize your oneness with all existence as AUM, the Cosmic Vibration.
>
> This state is known as AUM Samadhi, or union with God as Cosmic Sound.
>
> By still deeper meditation, one perceives in the physical body, underlying the AUM vibration, the vibrationless calm of the Christ consciousness, the reflection in creation of the unmoving Spirit beyond creation.
>
> By ever-deeper meditation, one expands his awareness of the Christ consciousness beyond the limits of the body to perceive his oneness finally with the Christ consciousness, which underlies the manifested universe.
>
> By deeper meditation still, one goes beyond creation and unites his consciousness with that of the Father, the vast ocean of Spirit.

# CHAPTER THIRTEEN

# Living in the Consciousness of AUM

O f all divine manifestations, Cosmic Sound is the most constant and easiest to commune with. Attuning to AUM's pristine vibration helps one understand that at the very center of movement lies stillness.

AUM is God's consciousness in vibratory creation. Every atom is a trumpet that proclaims His glory. In AUM one hears the Cosmic Symphony—played by every atom vibrating with God's bliss. The negative and positive forces in each atom resist each other and produce a quiver. The combined quivers from every vibrating atom in the universe produce the sound of AUM.

A former alcoholic—who before becoming sober meditated with his mala beads in one hand and a bottle of whiskey in the other—confided to Swami Kriyananda, "At work I hear AUM so loudly, it drowns out the noise from the factory machinery."

Behind every outer sound is the rumble of AUM. Swami Kriyananda recalls as a child riding in a car on long journeys: "I would close my eyes, and listen to the steady swish of the tires on the highway. After a bit, it seemed to me that I was hearing a symphony orchestra playing marvelous melodies." He continues, "My dome living room at Ananda Village exerted a similar effect on me. As I listened to the distant sounds of the river echoing softly in the room, musical creations came to me almost effortlessly." When writing music Swami Kriyananda always refers the melody back to the sound of AUM.

He writes in *Revelations of Christ*, "Many times, while writing this book, I have been entranced to hear that sound [AUM] within and around me, as if in divine corroboration and approval of what I had written."

## GRACE FLOWS
## THROUGH AUM

The physical world is a reflection of your consciousness. AUM, as the Invisible Mother, becomes visible to create a unique world for each soul. God is more personal than you think. God, Yogananda says, is talking to you all the time through vibration. His Cosmic Energy materializes the ideal environment for you to experience and overcome your karma.

Gaze at the world around you. Everything you perceive—trees, flowers, people, mountains, and buildings, even your own feelings—originate from AUM. Share with God as AUM everything you see, hear, feel, and do. Pray to Divine Mother: "Help me feel Your vibratory presence in all forms and atoms."

## THE POWER OF CHANTING AUM

"Through AUM the Lord is met face to face." (SWAMI SHANKARA) For millennia the core practice of many yogic traditions has been the constant chanting of and meditating on AUM.

"AUM is the soul of your breath." (SWAMI SIVANANDA) To immerse themselves in Cosmic AUM, many yogis chant AUM with every breath. Rama Tirtha describes the practice of AUM Japa (the constant chanting of AUM) in this way: one's "lips and throat chant it physically, the mind chants it intellectually, and the heart chants it in a language of higher emotions."

Chanting AUM transforms every atom in the body and awakens spiritual power. "Chant Om, Om. If you do that for a few moments, your whole being from head to foot becomes Light." (SWAMI RAMA TIRTHA)

Swami Sivananda poses the question, "Why is AUM used as the symbol for Brahma?" To understand why, he recommends the following experiment: "Chant AUM for one hour, then chant any other word for an hour. Afterwards, you'll feel the difference."

To feel AUM's holy vibrations in your whole being, Paramhansa Yogananda recommends saying AUM mentally in each body part and chakra.

During a severe kidney stone attack, Nayaswami Sadhana Devi experienced AUM's transcendent power:

> After three hours of intense pain, I realized its location was near the lower three chakras. As the stone made its way down through my body I began chanting AUM at the appropriate chakra. I chanted as loudly as I could and visualized light at the chakra. Each time I chanted, the pain decreased dramatically; each time I stopped, it returned in full force. I could feel AUM vibrating in the chakras, as though breaking up the stone. Finally, after a couple of hours of chanting, the pain stopped completely and never returned.

## THE SUPREME VIBRATION

Everything is energy in condensed form: plants, rocks, stars, and our bodies vibrate at different frequencies. "Because nature is an objectification of AUM, . . . man can obtain control over all natural manifestations through the use of certain *mantras* or chants. Historical documents tell of the remarkable powers possessed by Miyan Tan Sen, sixteenth century court musician for Akbar the Great. Commanded by the Emperor to sing a night *raga* while the sun was overhead, Tan Sen intoned a *mantra* which instantly caused the whole palace precincts to become enveloped in darkness."* (PARAMHANSA YOGANANDA)

On August 28, 2004, members of Ananda Village witnessed a dramatic demonstration of AUM's sovereignty over natural phenomena. Late August in California is the height of the fire season, with grasses browned by the summer heat.

At 11:30 a.m. a fire started on the steep slope below Ananda's guest retreat, The Expanding Light. The fire's location made it especially ominous. Forest fires travel much faster uphill than downhill, because the fire preheats its uphill fuel with the rising smoke and heat.

The blaze spread quickly and raced upward, threatening to destroy The Expanding Light and the Ananda Community. Nine air tankers and helicopters soon appeared and began dropping water and fire retardant. Forty fire engines and four hundred firefighters arrived shortly afterwards to try to contain the growing inferno.

As low-flying bombers released red streams of fire retardant into the thick, smoky air, the retreat look more and more like a war zone. Many community residents and guests were covered with fire retardant.

Everything that could be done on the physical level was being done. Government agencies had responded quickly and capably to the fire. Ananda residents were putting out spot fires, thus freeing the professional firefighters to work on the front lines of the

* *Autobiography of a Yogi.*

blaze. Fire crews were doing a magnificent job protecting the retreat buildings and slowing the fire's advance.

Despite the concentration of many fire fighting resources gathered to fight the blaze, the fire chief had the uneasy feeling that this fire was "going to be one of those that go totally out of control and burn thousands of acres and hundreds of homes." His concern seemed validated when the inferno began moving uphill toward a nearby cluster of twenty Ananda homes. With strong winds pushing the fire upslope, the blaze seemed more and more likely to reach the cluster. Residents of the threatened homes were already packing and evacuating.

At the Ananda Community market and visitor center, located a safe quarter-mile from the fire, retreat guests and community residents had gathered. Seeing that people were frightened—and feeling that Ananda was under psychic attack by a dark force that had manifested as the fire—Nayaswami Devi organized a prayer circle. The circle started with twenty people, and grew to fifty.

Those gathered blessed the fire fighters, the homes and buildings of our neighbors and of Ananda, the fire itself, and the trees and wildlife living on the land. After each prayer they chanted AUM three times, to energize their petition by the truth of Cosmic AUM.

The Cosmic Vibration is beyond duality. The swings of cause and effect (karma) are stilled and nullified by AUM's pristine vibration. "At first," Devi said, "the darkness seemed stronger than our prayers. But after two hours of praying and chanting AUM, the darkness felt diminished."

When the fire chief arrived back at the market area, he was quite pleased. The fire was contained. To the Ananda residents, he said, "You were very lucky. I have never seen winds reverse themselves so dramatically. The fire was heading toward the housing cluster when it suddenly stopped—because the wind suddenly changed direction. I don't know what you people did. But it worked."

Forest fires are only objectifications of AUM (albeit, rather exciting ones). Fire is one of the elements or vibrations through which AUM expresses and solidifies Itself in this world.

When you feel worried or anxious, call on Holy AUM. Pray believing in its sovereignty over matter. "Problems . . . that arise when we deal with inert matter will be transformed . . . once we become conscious that we are dealing with a living reality *behind* [matter]." (SWAMI KRIYANANDA) AUM *is* the living reality behind every joy and challenge in your life. It's the universal Cosmic Energy that creates, sustains, and destroys universes. AUM is the personal aspect of God—the Divine Mother—Who comforts all those who are receptive to Her sovereignty and love. Remember always Yogananda's promise: "When you are in the consciousness of AUM, nothing can touch you."

When Doctor Lewis, Yogananda's first Kriya Yoga disciple in America, was sailing outside Boston Harbor, a sudden storm blew up, with great violence. Thinking he might drown, he focused his consciousness at the Christ center in the forehead and saw the great light of the spiritual eye. [The inner light is a primary manifestation of the Cosmic Vibration.] Instantly, he felt a sense of peace and security envelop him, and he knew he would survive: nothing could harm him; he was safely in the consciousness of AUM.

"When I got home," Doctor Lewis said, "the phone rang. Master was on the other end of the line. He said to me, 'You came near getting wet, Doctor, didn't you?'"

## KNOW THYSELF

AUM is the mountain that every pilgrim ascends to merge into the rarified air of Spirit. You can sense AUM's omnipresence—and your descent from the Cosmic Vibration—by observing how easily musical vibrations influence you. "Because man himself is an expression of the Creative Word," Yogananda said, "sound has the most potent and immediate effect on him."

On a remote South Pacific island during World War II, a United States soldier heard the sublime music of Beethoven's Opus 132 playing in the night. As he listened to its glorious arrangement, he wondered how could any soldier who paused long enough to listen to this soul-stirring music could kill another human being.

The winds of grace are always blowing. A man from Massachusetts told me that, as an infant, he heard the sound of AUM continuously. When adults around him became worried or inharmonious, he wanted to comfort them: "Don't worry. Everything is okay because AUM is here." But he hadn't yet learned to speak, and so wasn't able to share with them the comforting power of AUM.

In 2011 Nayaswami Anandi and I visited Hiroshima's Peace Memorial Park. The park features a five-and-half-foot-high bell that visitors are encouraged to ring for world peace. Etched on the surface of the Peace Bell is a world map with no national boundaries—to symbolize a united earth. Melodious tolling of the bell—accompanied by the desire for peaceful co-existence of those who ring the bell—continuously reverberates throughout the extensive grounds.

Anandi and I were deeply moved to see people ringing the Peace Bell, an act which, to the yogi, symbolizes AUM flowing through the heart chakra. On the Peace Bell is written the words, "Know Thyself." When you truly do know yourself, you realize that you—and everything you see—are blissful manifestations of AUM.

The eight attributes of God—love, peace, joy, power, wisdom, calmness, light, and sound—emanate from Cosmic Vibration. Living in the consciousness of AUM is the highest way to serve others. Then AUM's thrilling bliss flows through your inner being and touches the hearts of all creation. "Meditate on AUM," Swami Rama Tirtha said, "and be a giver of peace to mankind."

ॐ

# KEEPING THE COMPANY
# OF AUM

### I.

Sit where there's an expansive view. Gaze into the distance. Then look at the picture below and meditate on AUM's qualities of eternity, infinity, and immortality.

### 2.

Swami Sivananda was a great devotee of the Cosmic Vibration; constant absorption in AUM was the heart of his spiritual practice. Read an excerpt of his poem below about finding God while sitting by the Ganges.

I sat alone on a block of stone
On the banks of the Ganges;
I meditated on Om and its meaning.
The little personality was lost;
The mortal limit of the self was loosened;
But there was infinite extension.
I entered the Nameless beyond,
No words can describe the thrill of joy,
The little "I" fused into the incandescent brilliance.
One Mass of transcendental light Bliss.

*—Excerpted from* Vairagya Mala

### 3.

Sivananda was often observed sitting quietly and tracing the symbol of AUM over and over again on his thigh. With gratitude and reverence, write AUM on your thigh and feel God blessing you through His Blissful Cosmic Vibration. With every tracing of AUM feel the joy of Divine Mother—your Beloved Comforter.

CHAPTER FOURTEEN

# *Play Thy Celestial Music Through Me*

nce a king lived in a palace surrounded by a large garden. The king's subjects often visited his garden to enjoy its many beauties. One day, a man entered the royal estate and kept walking until he reached the palace. There he asked to see the king, who greeted him warmly. Together they toured the grounds, and the king showed him how he'd made the garden. Other visitors had gained only a superficial understanding of the garden. But the man—who had been tutored by the garden's creator—knew it intimately.

Paramhansa Yogananda once had an extraordinary samadhi, in which the Divine Mother took him around the universe. "At one point Yogananda exclaimed delightedly, 'Oh, *now* I see how You do it!' She was showing him the mysteries of cosmic creation."
(SWAMI KRIYANANDA)

Everything in existence comes out of AUM and goes back into AUM. Cosmic Vibration creates all forms; the differences among solids, liquids, gases, mountains, and stars are merely differences in the rates of vibration. AUM bestows the highest states of awareness and the deepest knowledge. He who knows AUM knows all.

Life continuously changes. "Change is part of the vibration that keeps the universe going, because it is always moving from one opposite to another. If you could get into AUM during meditation you would have the greatest power to harmonize yourself with change, to gain the best from change, and to resist change when necessary. Because all change comes out of AUM, you'll find that when you are in AUM nothing can touch you." (SWAMI KRIYANANDA)

AUM is the creative power of the universe. It is the fountain of all wisdom and inspiration. "The best way to express this inspiration, is to listen inwardly to AUM, first, or to listen for it if you cannot yet hear it. When you hear that sound, thrilling to the soul, expand your consciousness with it until it fills your brain, then your entire body. Your creative efforts will become attuned to the highest source of inspiration, and will no longer merely express your own personal tastes and feelings. Your perception becomes attuned to the cosmic mind and is no longer limited to your individual self. Your intellect becomes a universal, intuitive intelligence and understanding." (SWAMI KRIYANANDA)

Cosmic Energy sustains universes. This power vibrates in you, too. AUM communion gives you absolute command over the mind, tremendous magnetism, and power for doing active works. In AUM you receive marvelous inspirations, intuitions, and revelations at will. One reputed siddhi, or power associated with AUM union, is mastery of cosmic energy and the ability easily to accomplish things in the physical world.

Pray to AUM before, during, and after every activity. Visualize God's grace flowing through AUM to bless everything you do. Feel the joy of the universe passing through you, and Holy AUM acting through and around you.

In AUM one transcends selfish action, and one's personal will unites with the Divine Will.

Every organ can produce beautiful music, especially so when played by a master musician. "The instrument is blessed by what flows through it." (PARAMHANSA YOGANANDA) Let the Cosmic Musician play His thrilling melodies through your soul.

God constantly speaks to you through Cosmic Vibration. He yearns for the day when every soul hears and merges into His vibrations of love.

# The Cosmic Fire

*"The householder leaves his house when he hears AUM."*

KABIR

The calmer you become, the more you'll hear and feel the vastness of vibratory creation within you. One's consciousness increases with expanding, all-spreading AUM to the shores of Infinity.

AUM is the sacred, inner fire. As you approach the cosmic blaze, you feel at first its radiant, soothing comfort; then, as you come closer—AUM's liberating flames consume you.

"Melt into AUM," Yogananda often told his disciples. Attuning to the Cosmic Vibration is the highway every soul must travel to find God.

# THE DAILY MEDITATOR:
## *Inspiration for Meditators*

Nayaswami Bharat often writes articles for Ananda Sangha Worldwide on meditation, which are featured in his popular blog, *The Daily Meditator*. The purpose of these articles is to help you meditate more deeply and regularly. (To subscribe to this free blog, go to: www.ananda.org/meditation/support.)

Printed here for the first time are some of the author's most beneficial and inspiring writings on meditation:

- The Joy of Interiorization
- Meditation Centers and Frees You
- How Should We Meet Our Tests?
- Contentment Is the Supreme Virtue
- The Mysterious Devotee: A True Story
- Why Hong-Sau Works

# The Joy of Interiorization

O n Japan's northernmost island of Hokkaido, I once led a winter nature outing for families. I still vividly recall an eight-year-old boy sitting quietly, intently writing a poem, while a downpour of thick snowflakes fell from the sky.

The boy was so focused that he was oblivious to the cold and to the snow piling up around him. The snow rose to cover his legs, then his waist, and still the boy remained virtually motionless. Everyone else had long since departed for the comfort of a large heated tent. Knowing the group was waiting for us, I asked the boy if he had finished his poem. "Not yet," he replied. Then he immersed himself once again in his poem.

The totally absorbed boy sitting in the white sea of snow made a strong impression on me. "To worship God 'in Spirit' means, in deep meditation, to rise above body consciousness." (SWAMI KRIYANANDA) The Japanese boy beautifully demonstrated the principle of one-pointed concentration so essential to deep meditation and to finding God.

The goal of meditation is to free one from physical and mental limitations and realities. In *Conversations with Yogananda*, Swami

Kriyananda tells how Paramhansa Yogananda could withdraw his mind completely from any pain his body suffered. Once, a thousand-pound concrete wishing well slipped from the grasp of the men lifting it, and crushed Yogananda's foot. Immediately the Master said, "I will show you something. I will focus my concentration on the point between the eyebrows." As he did so, every trace of pain instantly vanished from his face, and he could walk back and forth easily.

Nature's manifestations are often symbols for deep, inner realities. The sun, for example, is the most immediate "physical'" form of AUM, because it enlivens all life. Similarly, the awakened yogi's spine finds a physical counterpart in a river, because the human body also has a vast tributary system that feeds life-force into the central channel of the spine. Swami Kriyananda writes in *The Art and Science of Raja Yoga*: "Tremendous joy and awareness are experienced as one's consciousness becomes centered sensitively in the spine. The spine is, indeed, the holy river of baptism in which the Godward-moving soul becomes cleansed and regenerated in waters of divine joy."

There are instructive parallels between rivers and the flow of energy in one's spine. The Mississippi River's drainage area covers forty-one percent of the continental United States. After it has gathered the water from tributaries along its 2,350-mile length, its flow rate is tremendous—six hundred thousand cubic feet per second. At its headwaters, however, the Mississippi River is puny—flowing at six cubic feet per second. Thus, the river's volume is one hundred thousand times greater as it enters the Gulf of Mexico. The disparity in flow rate between the Mississippi River's headwaters and mouth is comparable to the difference between the energy flowing in the spine of an ordinary man and that flowing in the spine of an advanced yogi.

Most people's spines are spiritually paralyzed, and their life-force is locked up in their bodies. Spiritual progress begins when one redirects his energy inward—changing the center of consciousness from the body and senses to the spine and brain, and thus transmuting consciousness into superconsciousness. Withdrawing the life-force is the inner, universal path of all spiritual effort.

The goal of every raindrop is to reach the sea, just as it is the goal of every soul to unite with God. Both, however, must enter their respective "channels" if they wish to make rapid progress. Geologists estimate that it takes ninety days for a drop of water to travel the length of the Mississippi River to the point that it merges into the Gulf of Mexico. By contrast, if that drop remained in the earth as groundwater, it would travel just four inches per day. To journey the length of the Mississippi would take a hundred thousand years—over four hundred thousand times longer than by traveling in the river. Kriya Yoga draws one's energy into the river of the spine, and so is, as Yogananda puts it, the "super-quick" method for finding God.

According to yoga science, cosmic energy enters the body through the medulla oblongata, the negative pole of the sixth chakra, located at the base of the brain. Thence the energy moves down the spine and out through the chakras to different regions of the body. The energy flowing from the heart chakra, for example, radiates outward through the nerve channels to the physical heart, lungs, and chest, and into the arms and hands.

The spinal centers, or chakras, are found at the points where tributary streams of energy can flow either outward to sustain the body or inward from the physical body to the spine. There is a tremendous amount of energy locked in our bodies, waiting to be released. When it *is* released, the devotee feels an overwhelming sense of joy in his spine. "You don't realize how much power, bliss, and expansion there is in the chakras as you go deeper into them." (SWAMI KRIYANANDA)

To give you a greater sense of this subtle reality, practice *The River of Joy* visualization during your next meditation:

"Visualize your spine . . . as a mighty river flowing inside you. Feel its magnetic current rising upwards from the base of your spine to your spiritual eye and there merging into the vast Ocean of Spirit. Feel streaming into your chakras rivers of divine joy. Feel all of your chakras and your whole spine nourished by inflowing rivers of bliss. Pray: 'O Ocean of Bliss, I return to Thee!'"

Swami Kriyananda has defined Ananda as a rising flow of energy. The whole path of Kriya Yoga—devotion, selfless service, attunement with one's guru, meditation, and right attitudes—keeps your consciousness interiorized and expansive. God's nature is joy; and when the devotee, like the prodigal son, begins his journey home, he'll experience more and more of God's bliss in his life.

*"By following the trail of Om
you attain Brahman."*

SRI RAMAKRISHNA

# Meditation Centers and Frees You

While I was in New Jersey on a lecture tour, Thomas, my host, told how his meditation practice had helped him calm a potentially dangerous situation. Thomas is the superintendent of a small, rural school district, with three schools and 125 teachers. He had recently suspended the high school wrestling coach for verbally abusing his players. The suspension had been bitterly resented by the young coach and his large, extended family—so much so, that some of them had threatened Thomas with physical harm.

One Sunday, as Thomas was working alone in the district office, he observed four cars roaring into the parking lot. The cars came to a screeching halt in front of his building. Out swarmed a furious mob of the coach's relatives. As they charged into the building, Thomas called his daughter to notify school security. In the seconds remaining, Thomas centered his energy, and awaited for the approaching storm. And storm it did. His "guests" barged into his office, yelling, trying to intimidate him. Thomas sat quietly and weathered their rage. Seeing they couldn't scare him, they began vigorously stating the reasons why he was wrong. Calmly, and without fear, Thomas listened to their ranting, then quietly explained why he had done what he had.

During the confrontation, the relatives didn't want to agree with Thomas. They did, however, admire his courage and centeredness. They were very physical people, and they respected strength. Thomas's demonstration of inner strength won them over, and soon afterwards they not only accepted, but helped resolve, the situation.

The more centered one is, the more outer events adjust themselves to one's inner control, because centered energy is stronger than dissipated, reactive energy. Meditation helps the meditator to live from his center by dynamically bringing his consciousness into the spine. When one's energy is centered in the spine, he is in tune with God and with his spiritual nature.

## RESPOND TO LIFE'S CHALLENGES WITH HIGHER AWARENESS AND ENERGY

On another trip, this time to a small Ohio town, my host told me, "Recently the Ku Klux Klan (a white supremacist group) planned to march in our downtown area. "When people heard this," she said, "they were extremely upset. Many of our citizens and community organizations wanted to protest their march."

"Then a man in the town proposed a better response:

"'Instead of protesting the Ku Klux Klan march and giving them the publicity they desire,' he suggested, 'let's have a "Celebration of Community Day" at our park. With everyone at the park, there'll be no one to watch the Klan's parade. They'll be completely ignored.'

"And so the day turned out. On the day of the march, the townspeople gathered at the local park to celebrate their many religious faiths and ethnic groups and their appreciation and love for one another. Meanwhile, seven Ku Klux Klan members—in white, hooded robes—marched through the vacated downtown area. Except for one policeman designated to watch them, they were completely ignored. The marchers soon gave up and went home."

Like the townspeople, withdrawing their focus from the Ku Klux Klan, the meditator withdraws his energy from lower realities and lifts his consciousness toward higher, more expansive ones. The solution to all problems lies in higher consciousness, not in relating to problems from their own level. Albert Einstein said that the significant problems of today cannot be solved by the same thinking that caused those problems in the first place. When one reacts in kind to a negative or even to a mundane situation, he only perpetuates its consciousness.

One can never control outward events. One can, however, control his own energy. Lahiri Mahasaya's advice for overcoming any problem was always the same—to meditate more—because meditation centers and raises the consciousness and strengthens the aura. Meditation is the supreme tool for redirecting energy upwards to the superconsciousness. Yoga says, "Be a cause, not an effect." Meditate every day and you will begin to change your destiny and the world around you.

*"He who meditates on Om becomes a spiritual dynamo. He radiates joy, peace, and power to those who come in contact with him."*

SWAMI SIVANANDA

# How Should We Meet Our Tests?

wami Kriyananda was once asked why most people weren't interested in the spiritual path. He replied, "They haven't suffered enough."

Suffering encourages one to let go of attachments and limitations and to reach for something higher. Without pain, one wouldn't be motivated to seek further.

## "LORD, GIVE ME MORE SUFFERING"

Kunti Devi, the mother of three of the Pandava princes in the Indian epic, the *Mahabharata*, became sorrowful when her sons were banished to the forest. In her despair, she constantly repeated the name of Lord Krishna. After some time, her mind became free of sorrow and she began to experience an ever-present joy filling her soul.

Pleased with her faith and devotion, Krishna appeared to Kunti and asked what boon she would like—which of life's many pleasures could he bestow upon her. She replied, "Lord, give me more suffering, more difficulties, for it is in suffering that I remember you."

Tests come to the devotee for one reason only: To encourage him to seek his fulfillment in God. Paramhansa Yogananda said that for most people, a life without difficulties is a wasted life, because it contains little incentive to grow and take on a larger understanding. It is suffering that encourages one to reach for the divine within.

## TWO YEARS OF WORSENING SYMPTOMS

Illness is often one of the most serious challenges people face. It can be a major test. Twenty years ago I came down with a rare, debilitating illness: fatigue, fever, pain, and shortness of breath were my constant companions. Early in my illness, I was told my symptoms would eventually go away and my health would improve. During this time, I tried my best to heal myself through conventional and alternative medicine, and prayer. I also meditated as best I could.

After two difficult years of worsening symptoms, I had to ask myself honestly, "What if this illness never goes away?" I faced the very real possibility that it would be with me for the rest of my life. Then I thought, "I am going to have to change my consciousness!"

The purpose of tests is to encourage the sufferer to raise and uplift his energy level. If he simply waits out a test without raising his energy, the karma that caused the problem will again in the future sprout seed-like, and he will be right back where he started.

My illness lasted three-and-a-half long years. What did I learn during this time? The first lesson was not to become frustrated over what was happening to me, because giving in to frustration always led to despair. At times keeping frustration at bay was very difficult, but the more I succeeded, the happier I was.

The second lesson was to see my illness as God's agenda for me—at this time, right now. What was occurring in my life was not a mistake. I realized that I had to welcome what He was giving me. To the degree I resented or resisted it, I would be unable to see the situation clearly and thereby make the necessary changes.

Positive attitudes, service, and meditation practices enable the devotee to sail past most difficulties. But a serious test is designed to stop him in his tracks so that he will look at and discard attitudes and delusions that are holding him back spiritually.

What were the attitudes holding me back? Before the illness, I often evaluated myself by how much I served, how much I meditated, and how much good I was doing, particularly in giving lectures around the world. When I became ill, all that was taken away: I could neither serve nor meditate.

As a result of the illness, I learned not to define myself by anything outward. I went to the core of my relationship with Divine Mother and realized that She was satisfied simply if I loved Her.

The illness changed me in dramatic ways. I became more centered in myself and felt a greater sense of freedom and joy in all my activities. Cooperating with God's will during the illness enabled me to renounce personal desires and to live more fully for God.

Although the test was not easy, every day I am deeply thankful for it and for the invaluable soul lessons it taught me. Tests can be a source of tremendous blessing when one receives them in the right way.

## "MASTER, HELP ME TO UNDERSTAND"

Swami Kriyananda often says that the way to overcome tests is through love. He means that one must accept, and even embrace everything that comes. We should try to respond as did one of Kriyananda's brother disciples: when he fell off a ladder and broke his arm, he at once cried out, "Yes, Master!"

Another of Yogananda's disciples showed the same spirit under much more challenging circumstances. This woman underwent surgery for highly advanced cancer. When she woke up, the anesthesia had worn off; she was in tremendous pain and thought she might die.

Because she didn't want to die with the consciousness of feeling trapped in the body and identified with suffering, with all her heart and soul, as strongly as she could, she prayed to Yogananda: " Master, I have always tried to accept everything that comes to me as your will and for my highest good. Show me that this is true now. I'm not afraid of dying, but I don't want my life to end in this horrible negative consciousness. You cannot let me die like this!"

## GRATITUDE AND TOTAL ACCEPTANCE

Immediately she felt a calm presence surrounding her; inwardly she heard Yogananda say, "I will help you through this. The key is, be grateful for everything."

From the response in her heart, this woman knew that her gratitude had to be total—that she needed to be grateful for every tube that went into her mouth, for every intravenous drip attached to her arm, for every nurse and doctor, for every pain. What God wanted of her was total acceptance.

Practicing being grateful for everything was, she said, like climbing a ladder step by step. Even though she "was still in the darkness," she kept on thanking God for everything. After a few hours of effort she successfully climbed the ladder into a feeling of great light and joy. And she became a source of great inspiration to all the doctors and nurses in the hospital.

God comes to the devotee through all of his life experiences. As Swami Kriyananda explains, "Karmic law is an expression of divine love." A test is God coming to the spiritual seeker to reveal to him his limitations and to help him to grow and expand beyond them. Every challenging experience is his own lesson plan specially designed for him by God.

The way to overcome tests is to accept them calmly and pleasantly. It is reacting against challenging circumstances that increases their hold on you. When one can respond to tests calmly and cheerfully, he has successfully freed himself from identification with their reality, and so from their power to affect him.

## FAILING TO SEE
## THE FULL PICTURE

Usually one has no idea why a test has come because he doesn't see the big picture. The wrestling program I was involved in as a freshman in high school provides a useful example.

My school had just started the wrestling program and all of us were new to the sport. We began our first season with a week of intensive physical training. The technique we practiced most was the bridging exercise, in which the wrestler lies on his back and arches his neck to lift his back off the ground. We practiced this exercise over and over and were so sore afterwards that no one could turn his head without moving the entire body.

Being young and eager, we wondered when our coach would teach us how to pin our opponents. We thought, "Isn't the point of wrestling to win your match? Why are we spending so much time practicing this bridging pose—it's so painful!"

As it turned out, because we were new to wrestling and not very good, we spent most of our time on our backs with our opponents trying to pin us to the mat. We found that bridging was our best strategy. Knowing how to keep ourselves from being pinned allowed us to survive long enough to actually win some matches.

Life often follows a similar pattern. Because one often has no idea why certain tests come to him, he needs to face his challenges with faith and courage—faith that God knows what He is doing, and courage to embrace and work with what He sends.

Contact God in meditation so that you can experience Him as a God of love and joy. Then when trials and tribulations come, you will be able fully to trust Him and know that He is with you.

## BECOME A SPIRITUAL WARRIOR

A "spiritual warrior" is someone who fully accepts what comes to him. He understands that God is behind all of life's experiences because only God exists—nothing else is real.

From this understanding come liberating joy and freedom. Remember, nothing in creation can harm you when you live in the consciousness of God.

I would like to share with you a marvelous visualization for lessening (and even transcending) the intensity of karmic challenges. Karmic circumstances are a gift, specially crafted and designed by God for your growth and liberation.

When you face challenging or intense karma, use the following visualization to feel God's loving presence in the situation. You can also use this visualization before meditation and during the day to free you from something that is troubling you.

# EMBRACING YOUR KARMA

Karma is an expression of divine love.

Everything that comes to us is made especially for us by God—to free us from all limitation.

Visualize God as the Divine Mother, standing before you. (You can visualize Yogananda, or another saint if you prefer.)

See Her eyes gazing deeply into your own, filling you with Her love. Know that She is with you, always.

Think now of a karma that is challenging for you.

See Divine Mother holding before you this karmic test. See Her smile as she reaches out and offers this test to you with loving kindness.

Reach out *your* arms and take hold of this karma. Bring this karmic challenge into your heart.

Accept this precious gift—sent from the Wisdom of the Universe. Know that it is a perfect gift, sent by Divine Mother, to help your soul become free.

In your heart embrace this karmic test fully, with gratitude and trust. This karma can help you raise your energy level and consciousness to the level on which your Godly nature resides.

Focus now at the point between the eyebrows. See yourself rising to meet this karmic test and transcending its limitations.

See yourself becoming free in God. Feel the bliss of being united with Spirit.

*"The Comforter, who is the Holy Spirit,
whom the Father will send in my name,
shall teach you all things, and bring
all things to your remembrance."*

JESUS CHRIST

# Contentment Is the Supreme Virtue

*Whatever comes of itself, let it come, but*
*I am ever content in my inner heart.*

SWAMI KRIYANANDA

"When you can be happy in the present, then you have God." (PARAMHANSA YOGANANDA) I experienced the truth of these words one day after losing my way in the mountains.

It was late spring, and snow still covered the Sierra Nevada high country. While hiking back to my car, I went down the wrong side of a ridge and into unfamiliar territory.

When I realized my mistake, there wasn't enough daylight left to retrace my steps. Because I didn't have a coat it was imperative that I get to lower elevation and warmer, snow-free ground. I knew that continuing my present course would eventually bring me to a road—if not that night, certainly by morning.

Fortunately, when in my early twenties, I had already learned in dramatic fashion the importance of staying centered in myself. In Death Valley, friends and I were staying with the chief naturalist at the national park. I went for a long walk late one afternoon, going much farther than I intended. I realized that I couldn't make it home before dark.

I wasn't afraid, but because I was embarrassed that people might have to look for me, I began to jog back.

Twinkling lights soon appeared from the park staff's residences; I was still miles away. Then the night enveloped me, making it impossible to see my immediate surroundings. I had traveled cross-country, so there wasn't a trail to follow. I continued to run toward the far distant lights.

Suddenly, the sandy, pebbly soil gave way to hard rock. I immediately stopped; solid rock, I knew, might mean a cliff ahead. Peering into the darkness, I inched forward and tossed a rock in front of me. It took the stone too long to hit the ground: a rocky precipice was just ahead.

I realized how close I had come to disaster and was glad that I'd been paying attention. After feeling and searching with my feet, I found a steep ravine and carefully made my way down the thirty-foot-high cliff face.

After descending the rocky precipice—and breathing a sigh of relief—I had a revelation: I couldn't afford to worry about inconveniencing others. I needed to concentrate completely on my current surroundings and situation. Once I became clear about my priorities, the rest of the trip was uneventful.

Now, while descending the unknown ridge in the Sierra Nevada, I drew on my previous experience in Death Valley and felt completely relaxed. I realized that I might have some challenges ahead and might be bivouacking for the night. I focused my mind on God and offered myself into His hands. Knowing that fear and imagination often cause unwise decisions, I was determined to remain calm and centered in the presence of God. As I did so, I found my walk becoming more and more joyful, even though the daylight was nearly gone and the outcome uncertain.

Well after sundown I reached a large lake and began walking along its shore. When it was almost dark, I saw in the distance two men fishing from a boat. I wanted to ask them where I was but because yelling such a long way would disturb my inner peace, I kept on walking, feeling God's presence, which was only thing that seemed important.

When I came to a small cove, I saw another fisherman on the far bank. Now I was able to ask him in a calm, normal voice the name of the lake. "Spaulding," he replied, as he and his fishermen friends walked away. I was familiar with this lake; I now knew where I was.

Minutes later, as I cautiously made my way in the dark, I heard one of the fishermen ask, "Why don't you know the name of the lake?" To his direct question, I calmly explained how I had come to the lake by mistake. The man exclaimed, "But your car is twelve miles away, and it's nighttime! We'll drive you there."

My fisherman's friends disagreed with this plan, and I couldn't blame them. I was feeling so free and blissful inside that I didn't want the night to end. I sat in the backseat of their car, comfortably letting things unfold, as they discussed quite energetically whether to drive me or not. I felt perfectly fine with whatever they decided.

My friend and advocate eventually convinced his friends to drive me to my car. While driving my own car home that night, I felt deeply grateful to God for helping me experience the joy of accepting life's circumstances and not allowing time-consciousness to destroy my serenity.

## THOUGHTS ON CONTENTMENT AND THE ETERNAL NOW
### BY SWAMI KRIYANANDA

The more non-attached you can be in yourself the freer you will find yourself to be. The more you completely accept the present, the more energy will be released for you to enjoy the present.

How much is lost in life by people who perennially wish things other than they are! Who complain unceasingly, and tell themselves that the world owes them more than it is giving them!

Only by living properly right now, at the changeless center of the moment, can you arrive at that point where you exercise complete control over your life. Contentment has been said to be the supreme virtue. Contentment means living behind the present moment.

In God, no time exists; there is only now. The illusion of space and time is produced by movements of thought (restlessness). Without movement, Absolute Consciousness alone would remain.

*"Contentment leads ultimately to the realization of Divine Bliss in every atom of creation, even beyond creation.""*

SWAMI KRIYANANDA

# The Mysterious Devotee: A True Story

In September 2004, my wife, Anandi, and I welcomed a mysterious, unannounced visitor to our home. He stayed for eight days and thrilled us with his presence. Our "guest" spent his daylight hours sitting serenely in our meditation garden by a statue of Lahiri Mahasaya. Impressed by our visitor's dedication, we often looked out our bedroom window to see him still there, keeping his vigil by the saint's statue. Not knowing our friend's name, we decided to call him *Gurupod*, which means "at the feet of the guru."

Gurupod was a male deer, who for some inexplicable reason, came one day into our partially enclosed meditation garden to sit near the saint's statue. Gurupod had a wonderful presence, a calm disposition, and exuded a quiet strength. He was three years old and carried an impressive rack of antlers.

Resting in the garden, with the statue and fence right behind him, Gurupod was on his first day a little skittish when we went out to our small outdoor meditation temple. Because, to get there, we had to pass directly in front of him, we walked slowly, hoping not to frighten him. Gurupod's only reaction was to stand up, and walk thirty feet away with a leisurely gait, wait until we had gone inside the temple, then return to sit again near the statue of Lahiri Mahasaya.

Wild animals usually don't feel comfortable in an enclosed area when people are present, but Gurupod apparently was no ordinary animal. During the following days, as we walked within a few feet of Gurupod on our way to meditate, he would stand up as before, but now he walked only five to ten feet away before returning. As far as we could tell, Gurupod spent every moment of every day resting quietly by the statue of Lahiri Mahasaya.

Later in the week, I thought it would be inspiring to sit with Gurupod as I studied for a meditation class I would be giving. Gurupod, as usual, sat by the saint's statue, and I, on a small patio ten feet away. Although I was blocking Gurupod's only escape route, he remained calm and serene.

After spending several quiet hours together in the warm September sun, I turned to Gurupod, looked deeply into his eyes, and silently asked him, "Who are you? Have you come to teach me something? Have you come for Lahiri Mahasaya's blessings?" For a long time we held each other's gaze: Gurupod's eyes, calm and serene, and my own, inquisitive and grateful. I did not receive a definite answer to my questions, but I do know that Gurupod's poise and one-pointed focus have inspired me even to this day.

After our silent "conversation," it was time for me to meditate. On this occasion, Gurupod, after getting up as I walked by, did not return again to Lahiri's statue. Instead, he left the meditation garden and came around to the outer wall of the temple, on the side that our altar faces.

As I began my meditation, Gurupod continued sitting quietly in front of me, outside the wall, just a yard away. My heart felt so close to Gurupod that I wanted to do something for him. Swami Kriyananda has told us that if you want to relate to others spiritually, you should commune with them from your center to theirs. Kriya Yoga, because it centers your energy in the spine, is a marvelous way to pray for and bless others. The moment I started thinking of Gurupod during my practice of Kriya Yoga, he stood up and came right to the screened window where I was sitting, and looked at me from a foot away. Gurupod gazed intently at me the whole time I was dedicating my Kriya Yoga practice for his soul evolution. At one point I heard a few faint sniffs come from him. The moment I finished doing my Kriya practice for him, he again sat down by the meditation hut.

After my meditation with Gurupod, Anandi and I never saw him again. His first day with us was September 19th and he stayed until the 26th. Curiously, Lahiri Mahasaya's Mahasamadhi—a saint's conscious exit from his body—is on September 26, the last day Gurupod spent resting near the saint's statue.

Who was Gurupod? I don't know. However, I feel I can say truthfully that, on some level, Gurupod was magnetically drawn to the presence of Lahiri Mahasaya. His every action was a demonstration of that attraction. To me he was a thrilling reminder always to rest in the consciousness of the guru.

*"To listen to AUM is the only work
that has been appointed to man."*

LAHIRI MAHASAYA

# Why Hong-Sau Works

A friend of mine was organizing a large religious festival in which hundreds of people would be involved. Days before, he had wryly complained, "Even when I meditate, my mind is planning the event!" Meditators often find themselves in the same predicament: fighting an overactive mind with, seemingly, a life of its own. To meditate deeply, one needs to quiet the mind. The more he does so, the more effective his meditations will be. It's only in perfect stillness that one experiences the higher states of consciousness.

Swami Kriyananda wrote in *The New Path*, "Devotees attempting inward communion with God often find their efforts thwarted by restless thoughts. But long ago yogis found a technique for overcoming this obstacle. The breath, they discovered, is intimately related to the mental processes. A restless mind accompanies a restless breath. By simple, effective techniques for calming the breath, they found they could free the mind more easily for divine contemplation."

As the breath flows, so flows the mind, yogis say, because there is a feedback system between the mind and the breath. As the breath becomes calmer, so does the mind, and vice versa. In the practice of *Hong-Sau* we concentrate on the breath, and as we do so, the quieter it becomes.

The breath is the greatest obstacle to deep meditation. As long as there is bodily tension, heart movement, and brain activity, the body needs oxygen to purify the blood, a need which causes one to breathe. Physical activity, such as running, breaks down tissues in the body and causes decay; the result is a need to breathe more rapidly. Sleeping reduces physical and mental activity; the result is a lessened need for oxygen and a significant slowing of the breath.

The energy needed to keep the body functioning magnetically draws one into matter consciousness and restlessness. Every night one experiences the reverse of this principle when he sleeps. During sleep, energy is withdrawn from the periphery of the body and into the spine. This withdrawal of energy explains why sleep is so rejuvenating. This rejuvenation through sleep, however, Yogananda called "counterfeit samadhi," because sleep is a subconscious act, in contrast to meditation, in which one uses his conscious will. The direction of the flow of energy determines one's state of consciousness. Breathing techniques allow the meditator to redirect this energy inward so that he can experience a higher level of consciousness.

While many meditation methods ask one to concentrate on something outside of himself, the *Hong-Sau* technique asks you to focus on something *inside*—the breath. Since the mind is naturally drawn toward movement, the breath is a natural focus for meditation.

When you begin practicing *Hong-Sau*, you may notice first the mechanics of your breathing; but as your breathing becomes calmer, you'll be more aware of the breath itself. At this point, focus on the feeling of the air as it touches the inside of the nose. (If you consciously relax the inside of your nose, you will be able to feel the sensation of air more strongly.) As the breath becomes quiet, you'll feel this sensation higher and higher in the nose until you feel it at the highest part of the nose, at the point between the eyebrows. (An important benefit of *Hong-Sau* is that it directs the mind to the spiritual eye, but it is important not to divide your attention by concentrating at the spiritual eye before you feel the sensation of air stimulating this point.) In time, your breath will gradually diminish, until, finally, it is effortlessly suspended in breathlessness. The state of breathlessness may seem incredible to the rational mind. The explanation is that, when the body is totally still and no longer creating waste, there is no longer a need for the heart and breath to keep working.

The first time you notice that your breath has slowed down, or even stopped altogether, it's natural to feel a little anxious. Don't be alarmed—these pauses can't possibly hurt you, as long as you let the breath flow naturally and don't try to hold it in or out of the lungs by force. When your body needs to breathe again, it will do so. As you practice *Hong-Sau*, it will help you to try consciously to enjoy the pauses between your breaths. Remember: the purpose of *Hong-Sau* is to increase the intervals between the breaths naturally, and eventually to free you from body-consciousness altogether.

As a boy, Paramhansa Yogananda used to practice *Hong-Sau* for hours at a time, withdrawing ever more deeply into the spine until he found himself without breath altogether. *Hong-Sau's* three components—observing the breath, gazing at the spiritual eye, and mentally repeating the mantra (*Hong*, with the incoming breath, and *Sau*, with the outgoing)—all work powerfully together to draw the consciousness toward Spirit. Although it may appear to be a simple technique, in its simplicity lies its greatness.

Repeating the *Hong-Sau* mantra not only gives the mind a point of focus, its Sanskrit syllables stimulate the chakras and have a vibratory connection with the breath, thereby calming it. Yogis say that on a subtle level *Hong-Sau* is the very sound made by the astral breath. Gazing upward at the point between the eyebrows, the spiritual eye, puts you more in tune with the superconsciousness, where in deep meditation your energy will naturally be centered. Observing the breath helps to calm it; since the breath, as we've said, is the greatest obstacle to deep meditation, *Hong-Sau* works in the most direct way possible to bring you to a state of true meditation.

During *Hong-Sau* you are a *silent observer* of the breath. Do not try to breathe slowly or deeply; just let your body breathe as it wishes while you notice the flow of air. It may help you to feel that you are watching someone else breathe. Observing the breath without controlling it may at first seem a little awkward. But this awkwardness passes quickly.

The practice of not controlling the breath brings deep spiritual benefits, one of the most important being a sense of detachment from the physical body and mental processes. Every time you observe the breath without controlling it, you are affirming the attitude, "I am not this body." And every time your mind wanders, and you bring yourself back by repeating the *Hong-Sau* mantra, you are saying, "I am not this personality." Paramhansa Yogananda said, "The ego is the soul identified with the body." Patanjali, the great exponent of yoga, pointed out that when one no longer identifies with his one little body, he experiences himself in all bodies. Swami Kriyananda tells of the time he was helping Yogananda walk in the desert while the Master was in a deep state of God-consciousness. To explain his difficulty walking, Yogananda said, "I am in so many bodies, it is difficult for me to remember which body I am supposed to keep moving."

If you find yourself struggling with unruly thoughts during your *Hong-Sau* practice, know that every time you bring your attention back to the technique, you are helping to free your soul of its identification with the breath and the body. At the same time, you are strengthening your ability to concentrate. Concentration is like a muscle: the more you exercise it, the stronger it becomes.

Using the *Hong-Sau* technique to discipline your mind will bring you a great sense of peace and clarity. You will find that you can think more clearly and efficiently, and therefore work more quickly. Holding onto the deep calmness you feel from meditation will enable you to apply that peace to all of your activities and relationships. Besides the many spiritual benefits you'll receive from your *Hong-Sau* practice, you will discover countless physical and mental benefits as well.

While visualizations, affirmations, and many modern meditation and relaxation practices are extremely beneficial, the *Hong-Sau* technique is unique in that it has the potential to take you to God. Yogananda said this technique is "the greatest contribution of India's spiritual science to the world," and that one-hour of *Hong-Sau* practice equals twenty-four hours of sitting in the silence. One of the most sacred and ancient of all yoga practices, *Hong-Sau* is one of the four main techniques that comprise the path of Kriya Yoga, which Paramhansa Yogananda brought to the West in 1920.

*"Chant Om, Om. If you do that
for a few moments, your whole being
from head to foot becomes Light."*

SRI RAMA TIRTHA

# United in AUM

A friend of mine, as a child, spent a lot of time outdoors. When she sat still, nature's outer sounds would sometimes recede and she would hear the sacred hum of AUM. At such times AUM would silence her thoughts and bestow blessings of joyous serenity. In Holy AUM, she had found the ultimate sanctuary.

*"Seek the sound that never ceases."* When I walk in beautiful natural places, I often use these words of Rumi as a mantra to help me feel AUM's living presence in all forms and appearances: sparkling ripples on the pond's surface, bees buzzing, leaves crunching underfoot, stately trees reaching into the sky.

During mountain storms, John Muir loved to listen to the wind roaring through the trees. Often, after the winds had ceased and the forest was quiet again, Muir's inner ear could still hear the trees singing their songs. Every hidden cell, he proclaimed, throbs with music and life.

If one thinks of God throughout the day, he feels God more easily in meditation. Thinking of AUM throughout the day makes AUM more real to one's consciousness.

*Listening* to AUM attunes one to the causative, pristine vibration animating all forms.

# *O Holy Om!*

PARAMHANSA YOGANANDA

*O holy Vibration, boom on the shores of my consciousness. Reverberate through my body, mind, and soul, surroundings, cities, the earth, the planets, the universe, and every particle of creation. Unite my consciousness with the cosmic consciousness.*

*Teach me to hear Thy voice, O Father, the cosmic voice that commanded all vibration to spring forth. Appear to me as Om, Om, the cosmic song of all sound.*

*O omnipresent cosmic sound of Om, reverberate through me, expanding my consciousness from the body to the universe, and teach me to feel in Thee the all-permeating perennial bliss.*

*O cosmic sound of Om, guide me, be with me, lead me from darkness to light.*

# ACKNOWLEDGEMENTS

First, I would like to express my veneration to Holy AUM, the Mother of us all. May all Her children return to Her blissful omnipresence.

Second, I offer my gratitude and deep appreciation to my guru, Paramhansa Yogananda, and to my teacher, Swami Kriyananda, for their loving guidance. Yogananda brought to the West the essence of ancient India's teachings on meditation. Often while meditating I have felt his guidance showing me how to express AUM's subtle truths clearly and joyfully.

It has been my great fortune to live with Swami Kriyananda, a man immersed in Cosmic AUM. His blissful example of love, dedication, and attunement with God and Guru has inspired me for nearly forty years. I also bow with gratitude and heartfelt appreciation to all great saints and lovers of AUM, many of whom are included in this book.

I am grateful to Nayaswamis Jyotish and Devi for their support these many years; to Nayaswami Naidhruva for her encouragement; and to Nayaswami Prakash for editing the final manuscript.

Last, I would like to thank Nayaswami Anandi for her invaluable advice, support, editing, and total commitment to this book.

Thanks to all the photographers, including Swami Kriyananda, Nayaswami Jyotish, Sharing Nature Worldwide, Barbara Bingham, Robert Frutos, Akio Shoji, Alessandro Rovelli, Tejindra Scott Tully, and also to David Baron for making his deer photo public on the Creative Commons.

For the graphic use of her charming AUM charm throughout the book, I'd like to thank Beth Hemmila of Hint Jewelry; for more see bethhemmila.com.

# INDEX

FURTHER RESOURCES TO HELP YOU FIND

AUM

# SUGGESTED READING

*Autobiography of a Yogi*, by Paramhansa Yogananda, Crystal Clarity Publishers, Nevada City, CA, 1946

*The Essence of the Bhagavad Gita, Explained by Paramhansa Yogananda*, As Remembered by His Disciple, Swami Kriyananda, Crystal Clarity Publishers, Nevada City, CA, 2006

*Revelations of Christ, Proclaimed by Paramhansa Yogananda*, Presented by his disciple, Swami Kriyananda, Crystal Clarity Publishers, Nevada City, CA, 2007

*Meditation on OM and Mandukya Upanishad*, by Swami Sivananda, The Divine Life Society, Tehri-Garhwal, U. P., Himalayas, India, 1997

*The Story of Swami Rama Tirtha*, by Puran Singh, available free online

# AUM SEMINARS & RETREATS

*~ Presented by Ananda ~*

Nayaswami Bharat and experienced Ananda Meditation teachers are available to give lectures, seminars, and retreats on the art and science of listening to AUM. These programs, as well as this book, are based on the universal teachings of Paramhansa Yogananda and Swami Kriyananda.

Nayaswami Bharat has designed these programs to be philosophically thrilling, experiential, and deeply inspiring. Key components include music, meditation, and, where appropriate, outdoor exercises for communing with AUM.

If your organization is interested in hosting a program, email us at: aum.seminars@ananda.org or call us at 800-424-1055, outside US 530-478-7600.

Sharing Nature®

WORLDWIDE

## THE NATURE AWARENESS WORK

OF JOSEPH BHARAT CORNELL

Nayaswami Bharat is the founder and president of Sharing Nature Worldwide, one of the planet's most widely respected nature awareness programs. He is the honorary president of Japan Sharing Nature Association, which has 224 regional associations and 10,000 members.

He is also the author of the *Sharing Nature* Book Series,

used by millions of parents, educators, naturalists, and youth and religious leaders all over the world. Mr. Cornell's second book, *Listening to Nature*, has inspired thousands of adults to deepen their relationship with nature.

The U.S. Fish & Wildlife Service selected Bharat's first book, *Sharing Nature with Children,* as one of the fifteen most influential books pub-

lished since 1890 for connecting children to nature.

Cornell's highly effective outdoor learning strategy, Flow Learning™, was featured by the U.S. National Park Service as one of five recommended learning theories, along with the works of Maria Montessori, Howard Gardner, John Dewey, and Jean Piaget.

Mr. Cornell has received many international awards for his Sharing Nature books and work. He has received the prestigious Countess Sonja-Bernadotte Prize in Germany for his vast influence on environmental education in Central Europe. In 2011 Cornell was selected as one of the "100 biggest opinion leaders committed to the Environment" by the French organization, Les Anges Gardiens de la Planète.

## SHARING NATURE
## WELLNESS PROGRAM

John Muir said, "Nature's peace flows into us as sunshine flows into trees." Nature, the great healer, offers gifts of joyful serenity and vitality to every receptive heart.

During a Sharing Nature Wellness program you'll practice nature meditation exercises to quiet your mind, expand your consciousness, and open your heart to all creation. You will learn how to internalize your experience of nature and feel more at peace with life.

You'll delight in joyful nature awareness activities, feel more positive and affirmative, and feel a spirit of community and communion with others and with nature.

Nature's benevolent presence will remind you of life's higher priorities.

Sharing Nature Wellness programs provide uplifting experiences and healing through nature for individuals, and for leaders in business, education, religion, and the public sector. Courses can include instruction in meditation if desired.

To sponsor a program or find out more about Sharing Nature, visit us at www.sharingnature.com, or contact us at:

Sharing Nature Worldwide
14618 Tyler Foote Road BOX 210
Nevada City, CA 95959
PHONE: (530) 478-7650
EMAIL: info@sharingnature.com

# FURTHER EXPLORATIONS WITH CRYSTAL CLARITY

## AUTOBIOGRAPHY OF A YOGI

*The original 1946 unedited edition of Paramhansa Yogananda's spiritual masterpiece*

*Autobiography of a Yogi* is one of the best-selling Eastern philosophy titles of all time, with millions of copies sold, named one of the best and most influential books of the twentieth century. This highly prized reprinting of the original 1946 edition is the only one available free from textual changes made after Yogananda's death.

## PARAMHANSA YOGANANDA

**A Biography with Personal Reflections and Reminiscences** • *Swami Kriyananda*

Paramhansa Yogananda's classic *Autobiography of a Yogi* is more about the saints Yogananda met than about himself. Now, one of Yogananda's few remaining direct disciples relates the untold story of this great spiritual master and world teacher: his teenage miracles, his challenges in coming to America, his national lecture campaigns, his struggles to fulfill his world-changing mission amid incomprehension and painful betrayals, and his ultimate triumphant achievement.

## THE NEW PATH

My Life with Paramhansa Yogananda • *Swami Kriyananda*

*Winner of the 2010 Eric Hoffer Award for Best Self-Help / Spiritual Book*
*Winner of the 2010 USA Book News Award for Best Spiritual Book*

This is the moving story of Kriyananda's years with Paramhansa Yogananda, India's emissary to the West and the first yoga master to spend the greater part of his life in America. Through more than four hundred stories of life with Yogananda, we tune in more deeply to this great master and to the teachings he brought to the West. This book is an ideal complement to *Autobiography of a Yogi*.

## THE ESSENCE OF THE BHAGAVAD GITA

Explained by Paramhansa Yogananda • *As Remembered by his disciple, Swami Kriyananda*

This revelation of India's best-loved scripture approaches it from a fresh perspective, showing its deep allegorical meaning and its down-to-earth practicality. The themes presented are universal: how to achieve victory in life in union with the divine; how to prepare for life's "final exam," death, and what happens afterward; and how to triumph over all pain and suffering.

## REVELATIONS OF CHRIST

Proclaimed by Paramhansa Yogananda • *Presented by his disciple, Swami Kriyananda*

This galvanizing book, presenting the teachings of Christ from the experience and perspective of Paramhansa Yogananda, finally offers the fresh perspective on Christ's teachings for which the world has been waiting. This work offers us an opportunity to understand and apply the Scriptures in a more reliable way than any other: by studying under those saints who have communed directly, in deep ecstasy, with Christ and God.

## MEDITATION FOR STARTERS

*Swami Kriyananda*

Filled with easy-to-follow instructions, beautiful guided visualizations, and answers to important questions on meditation, the book includes: what meditation is (and isn't); how to relax your body and prepare yourself for going within; and techniques for interiorizing and focusing the mind.

## GOD IS FOR EVERYONE

Inspired by Paramhansa Yogananda • *Swami Kriyananda*

This book presents a concept of God and spiritual meaning that will broadly appeal to everyone, from the most uncertain agnostic to the most fervent believer. Clearly and simply written, thoroughly non-sectarian and non-dogmatic in its approach, *God Is for Everyone* is the perfect introduction to the spiritual path.

## CRYSTAL CLARITY PUBLISHERS

Crystal Clarity Publishers offers many additional resources to assist you in your spiritual journey, including many other books, a wide variety of inspirational and relaxation music composed by Swami Kriyananda, and yoga and meditation videos. To request a catalog, place an order for the above products, or to find out more information, please contact us at:

Crystal Clarity Publishers / www.crystalclarity.com
14618 Tyler Foote Rd. / Nevada City, CA 95959
TOLL FREE: 800.424.1055 or 530.478.7600 / FAX: 530.478.7610
EMAIL: clarity@crystalclarity.com

*For our online catalog, complete with secure ordering, please visit our website.*

## ANANDA WORLDWIDE

Ananda Sangha, a worldwide organization founded by Swami Kriyananda, offers spiritual support and resources based on the teachings of Paramhansa Yogananda. There are Ananda spiritual communities in Nevada City, Sacramento, Palo Alto, and Los Angeles, California; Seattle, Washington; Portland and Laurelwood, Oregon; as well as a retreat center and European community in Assisi, Italy, and communities near New Delhi and Pune, India. Ananda supports more than 140 meditation groups worldwide.

*For more information about Ananda Sangha, communities, or meditation groups near you, please call 530.478.7560 or visit www.ananda.org.*

## THE EXPANDING LIGHT

Ananda's guest retreat, The Expanding Light, offers a varied, year-round schedule of classes and workshops on yoga, meditation, and spiritual practice. You may also come for a relaxed personal renewal, participating in ongoing activities as much or as little as you wish. The beautiful serene mountain setting, supportive staff, and delicious vegetarian food provide an ideal environment for a truly meaningful, spiritual vacation.

*For more information, please call 800.346.5350 or visit www.expandinglight.org.*